06 Vienna , Paris , Aix en Provence , Rom Budapest , Lake Constance Zurich (Black/white/ gray)
Arya Bahram Art Photos Collection

عکس های هنری از آریا بهرام (مجید بهرام بیگی)

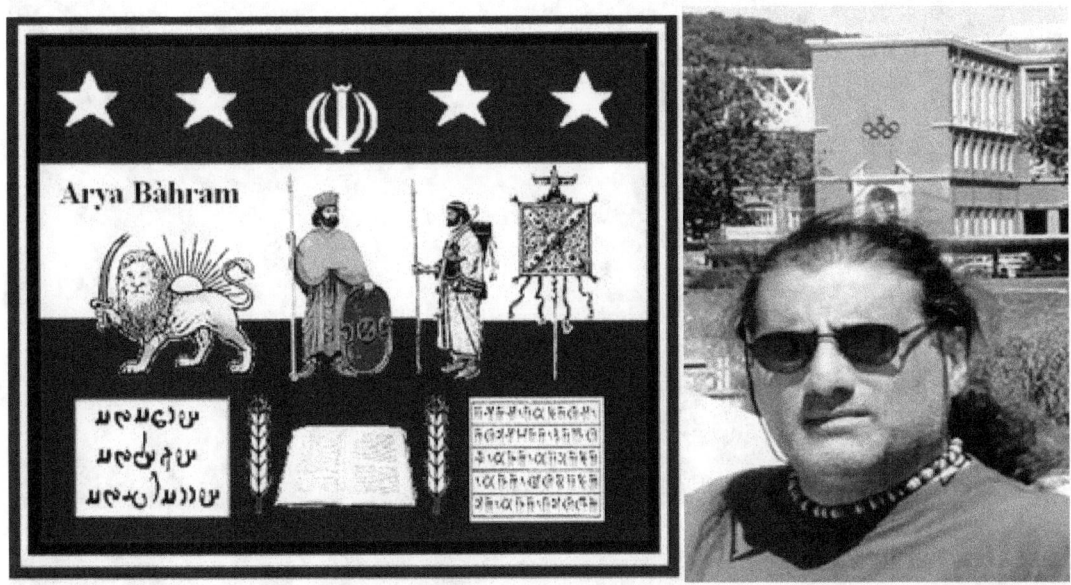

Musics for book - musiques pour livre - Musiken für Buch – آهنگها برای کتاب - Ahàng ha bàraye nibig ha

http://www.majidbahrambeiguy.at/my-foto-books---mes-livres-des-photos-.html

Arya Bàhram (Màjid Bàhram beiguy) , Österreich

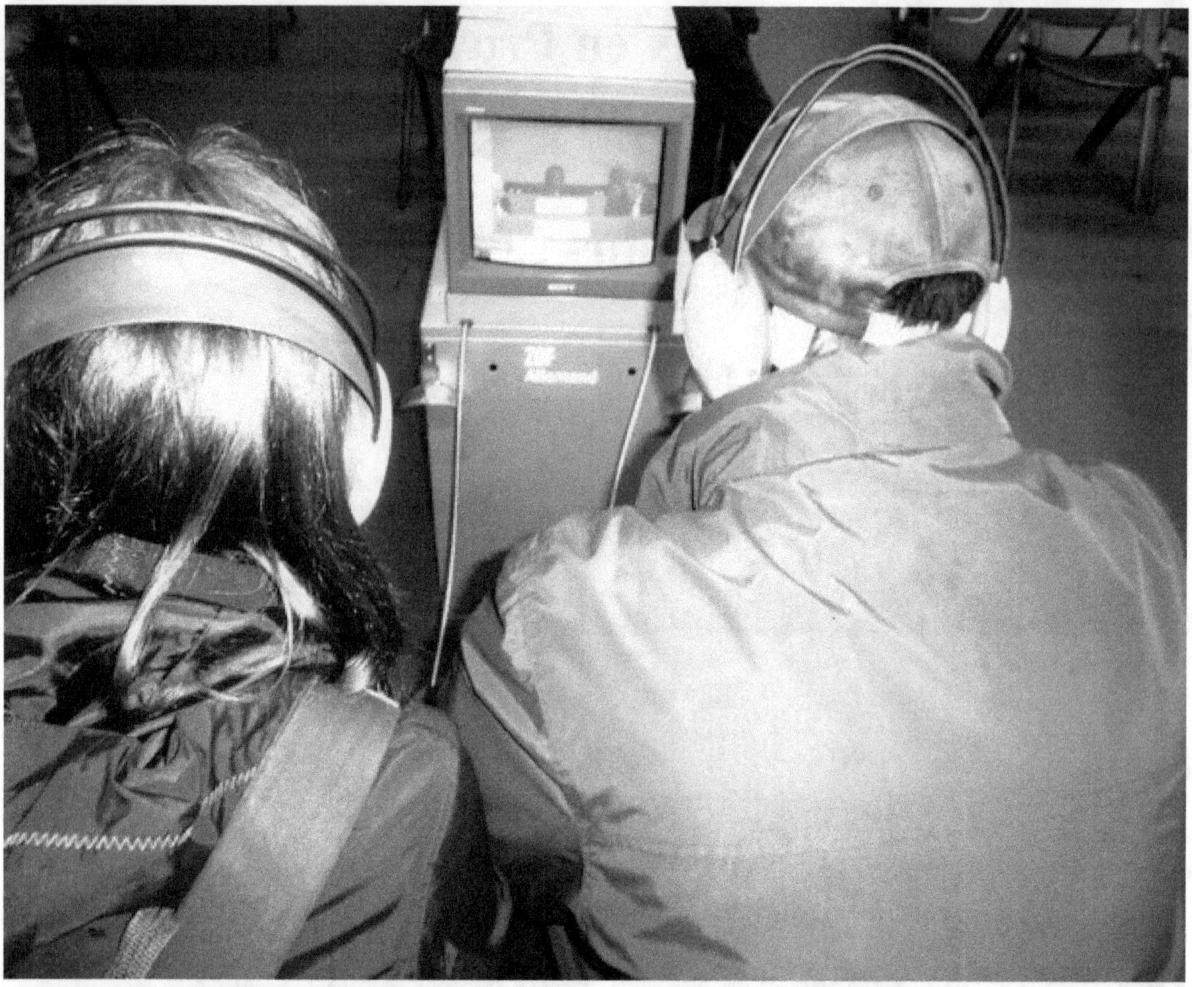

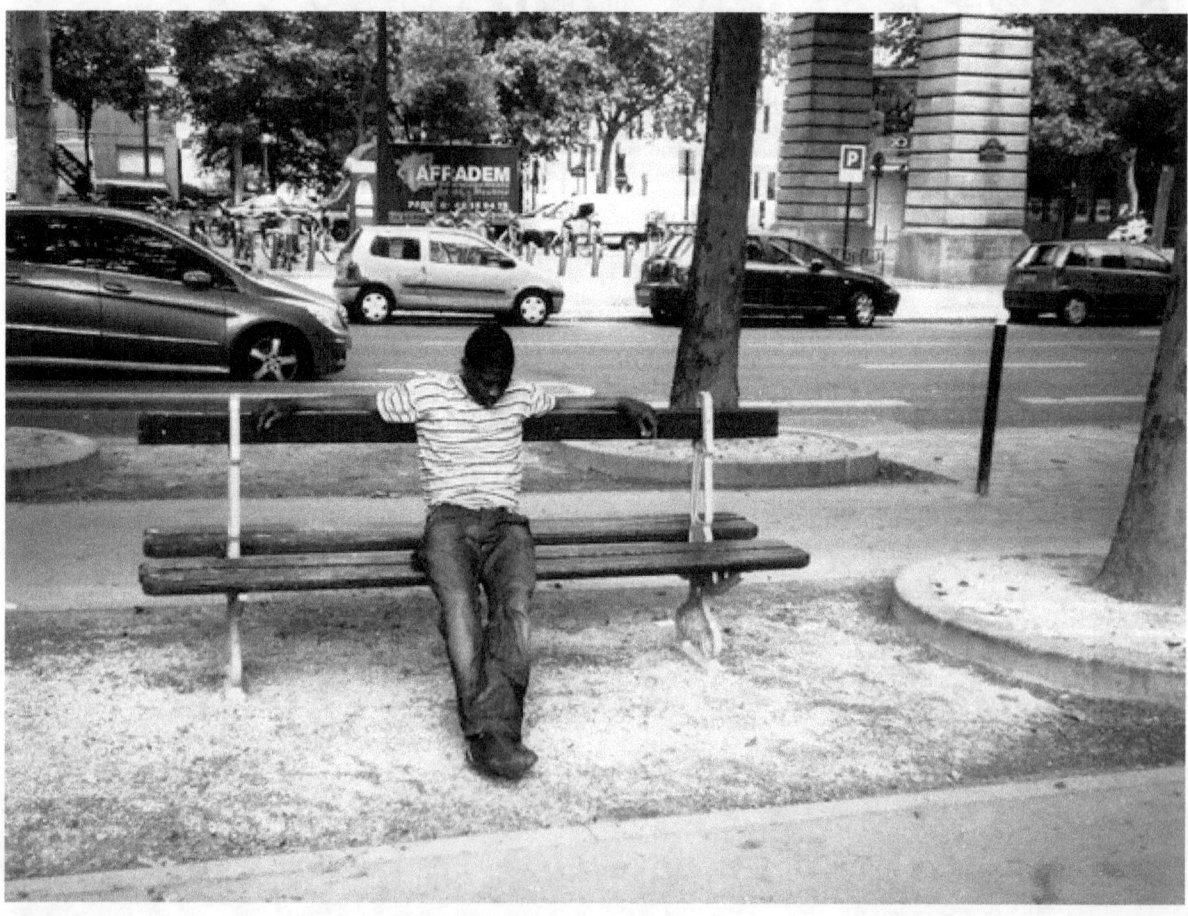

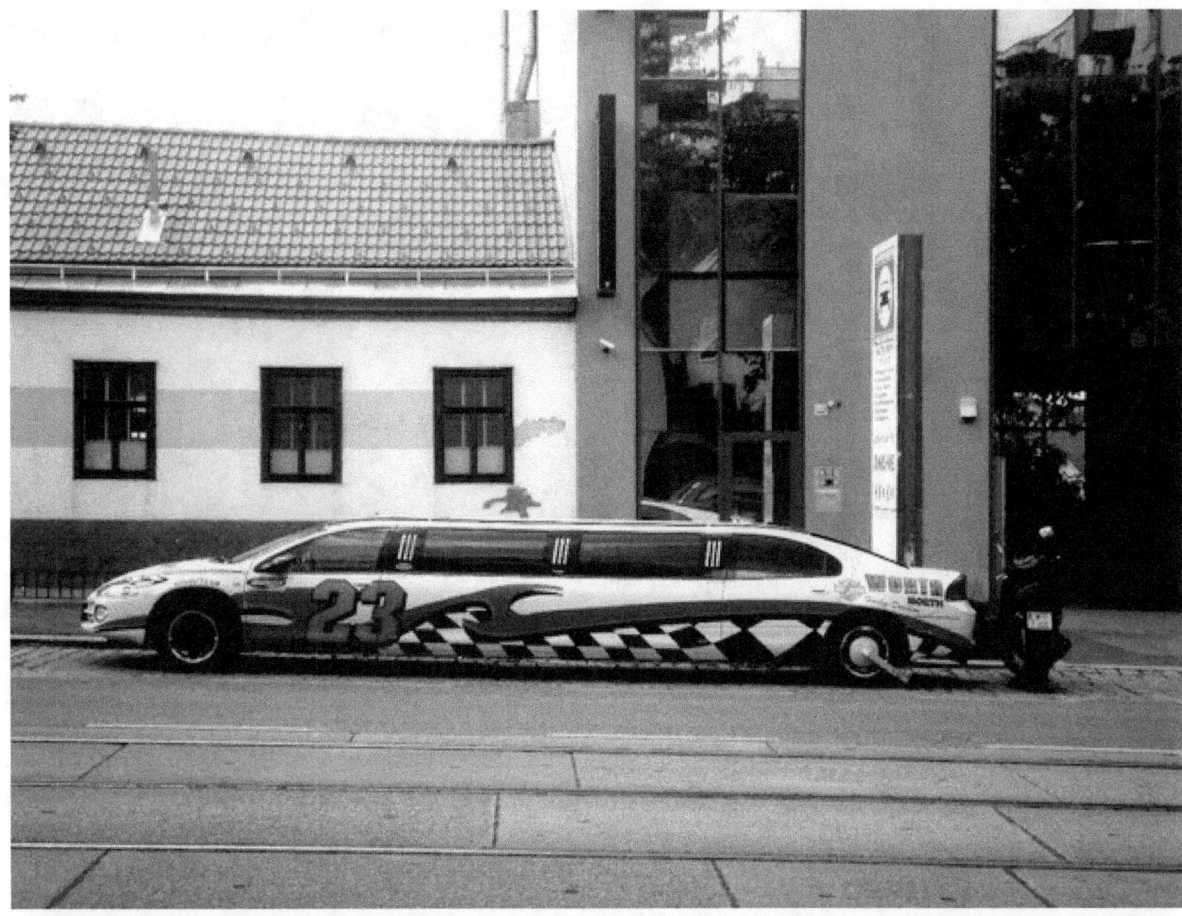

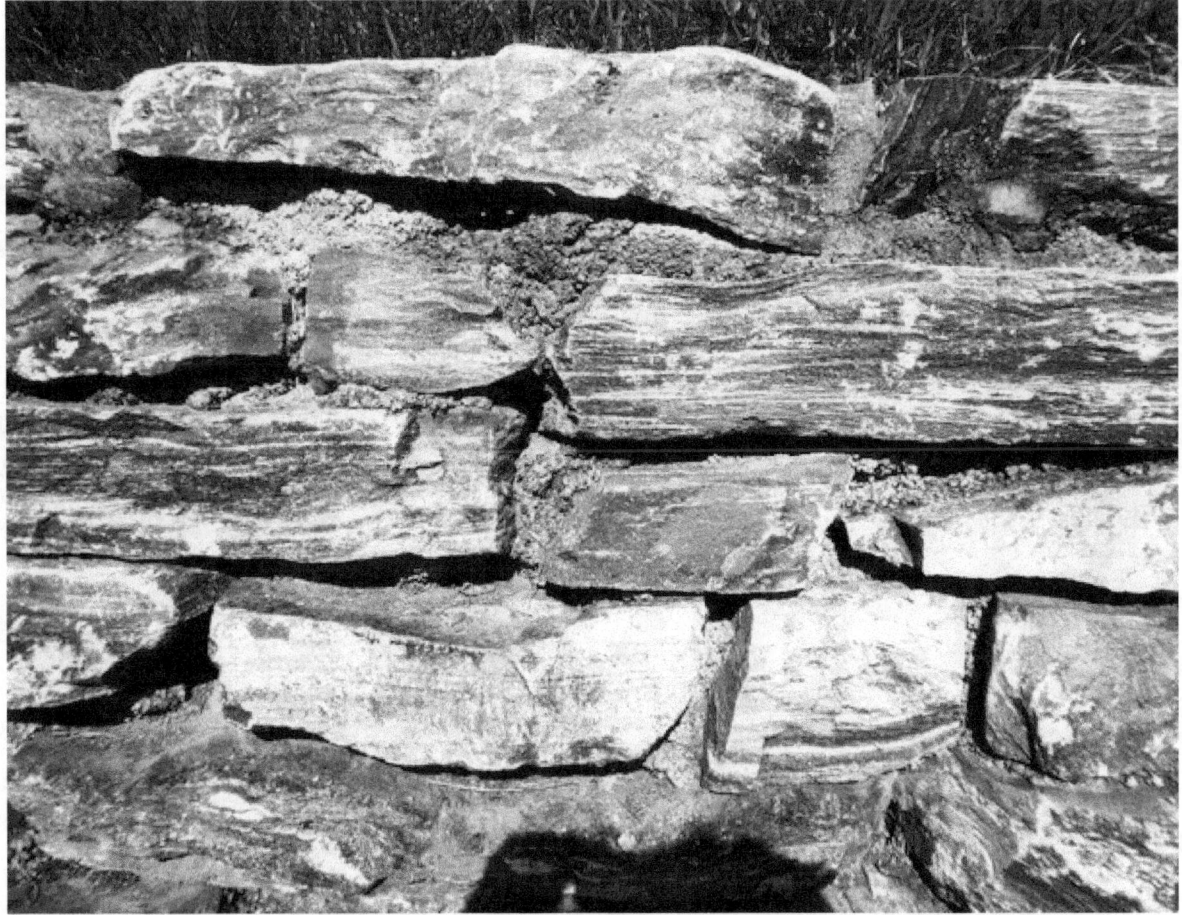

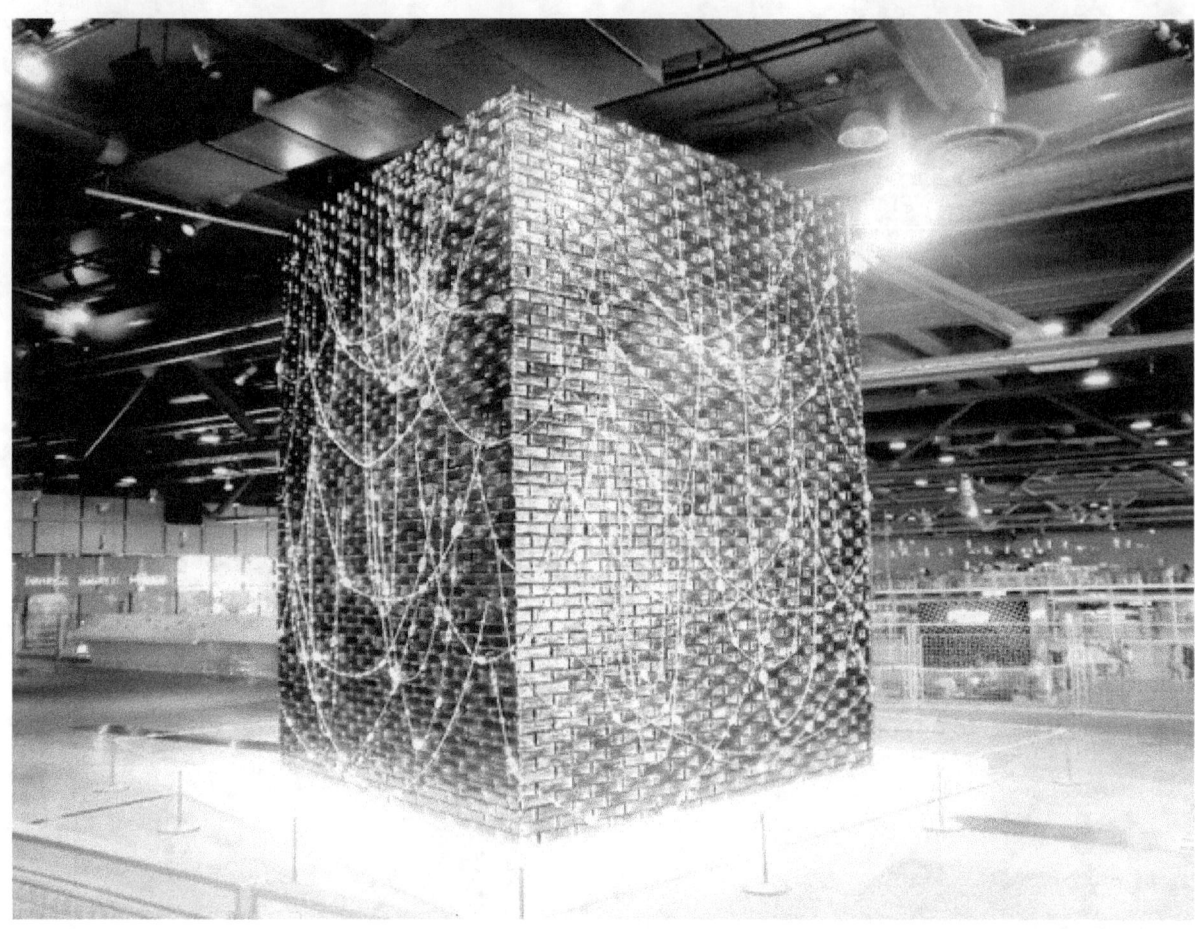

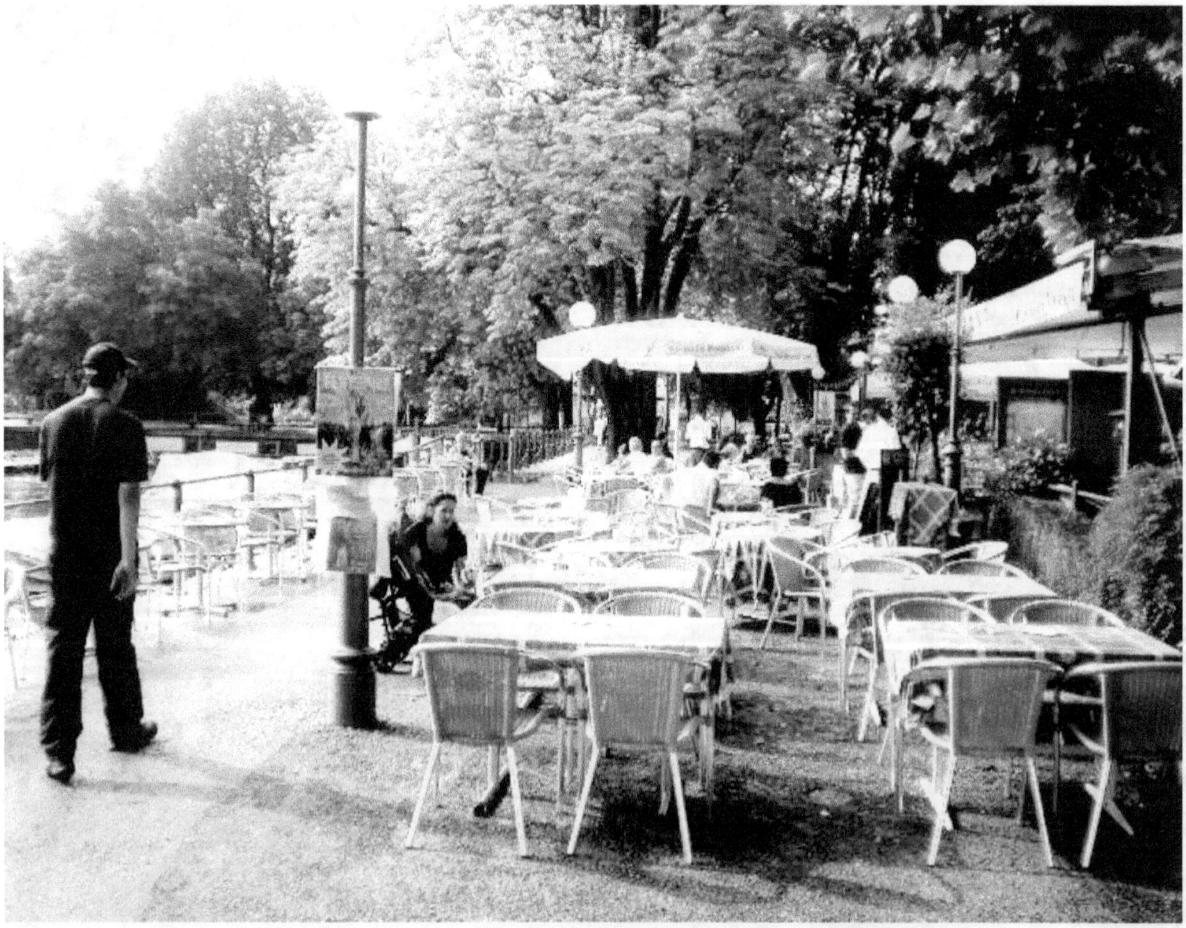

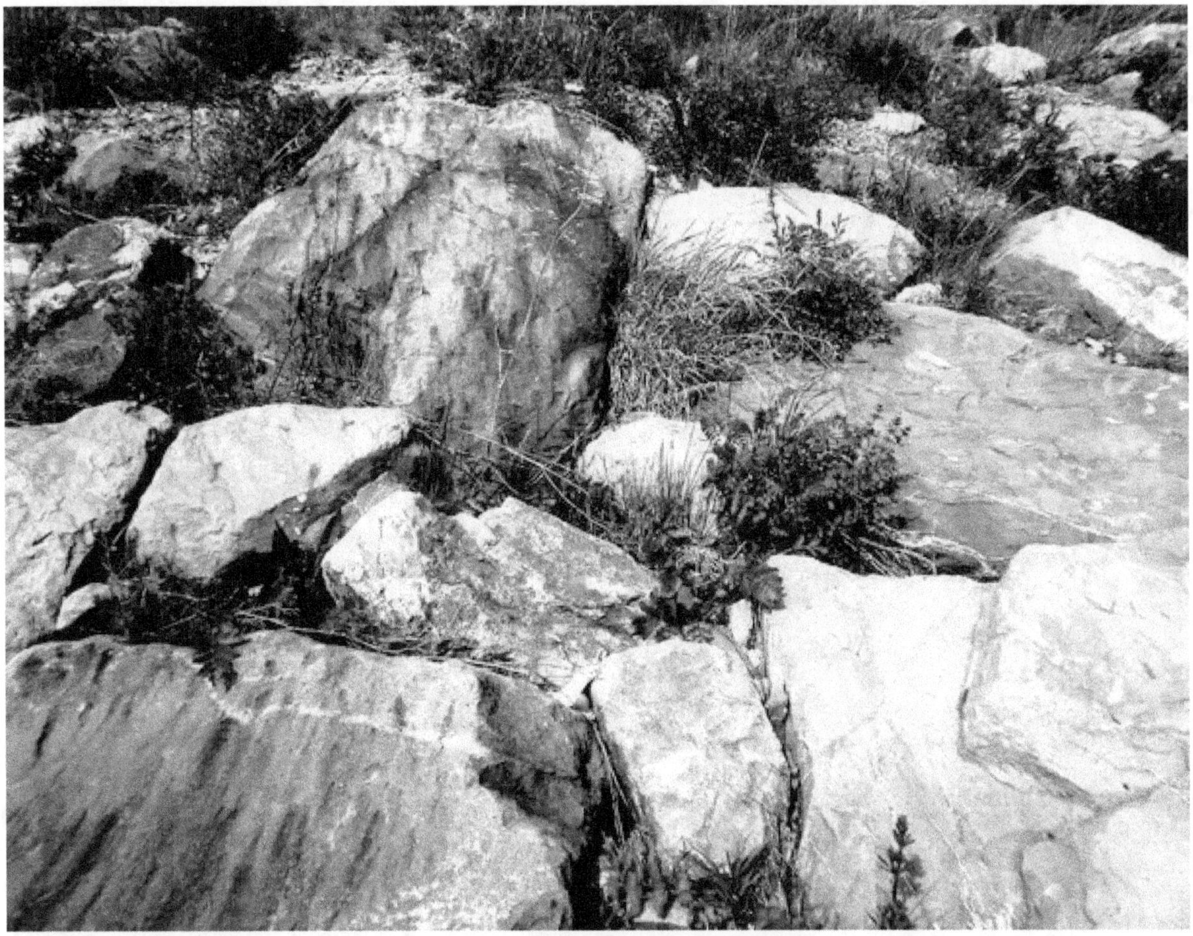

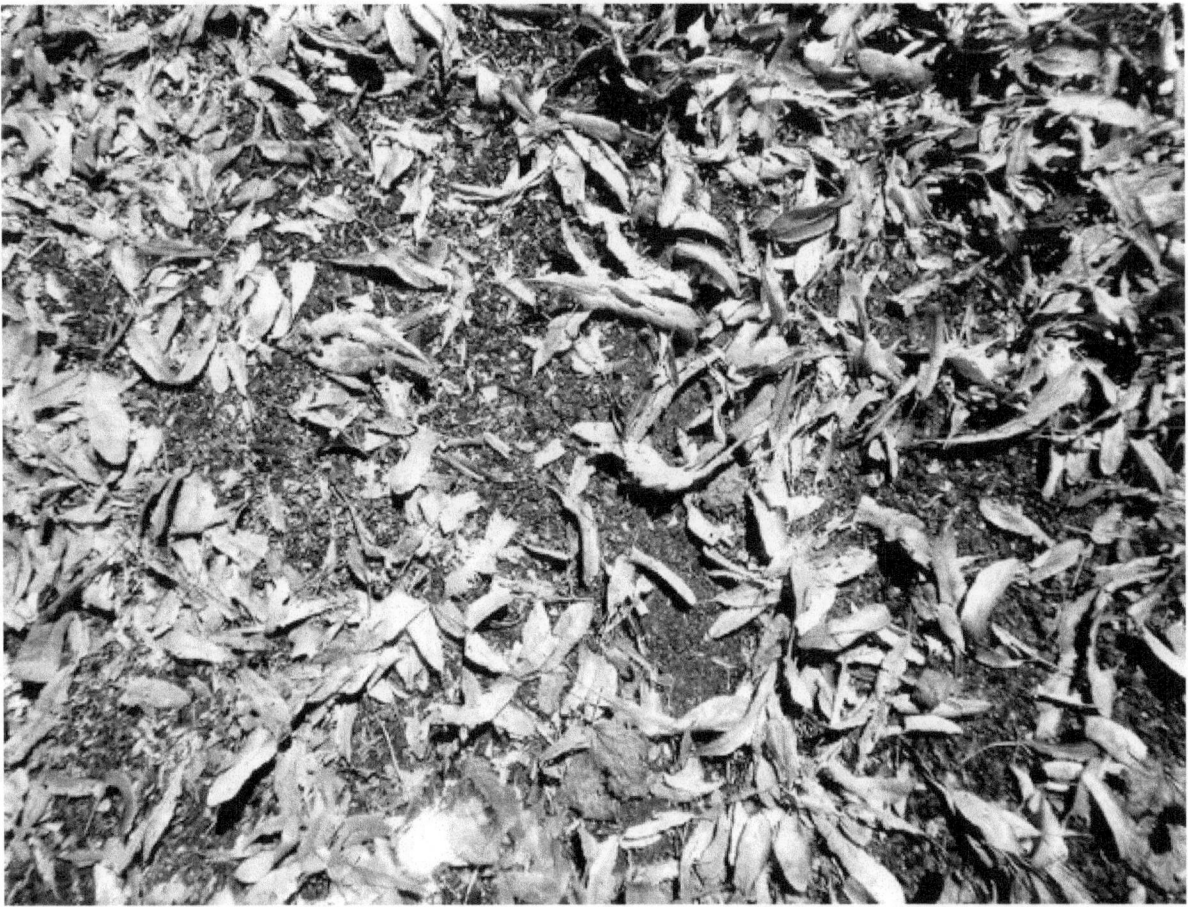

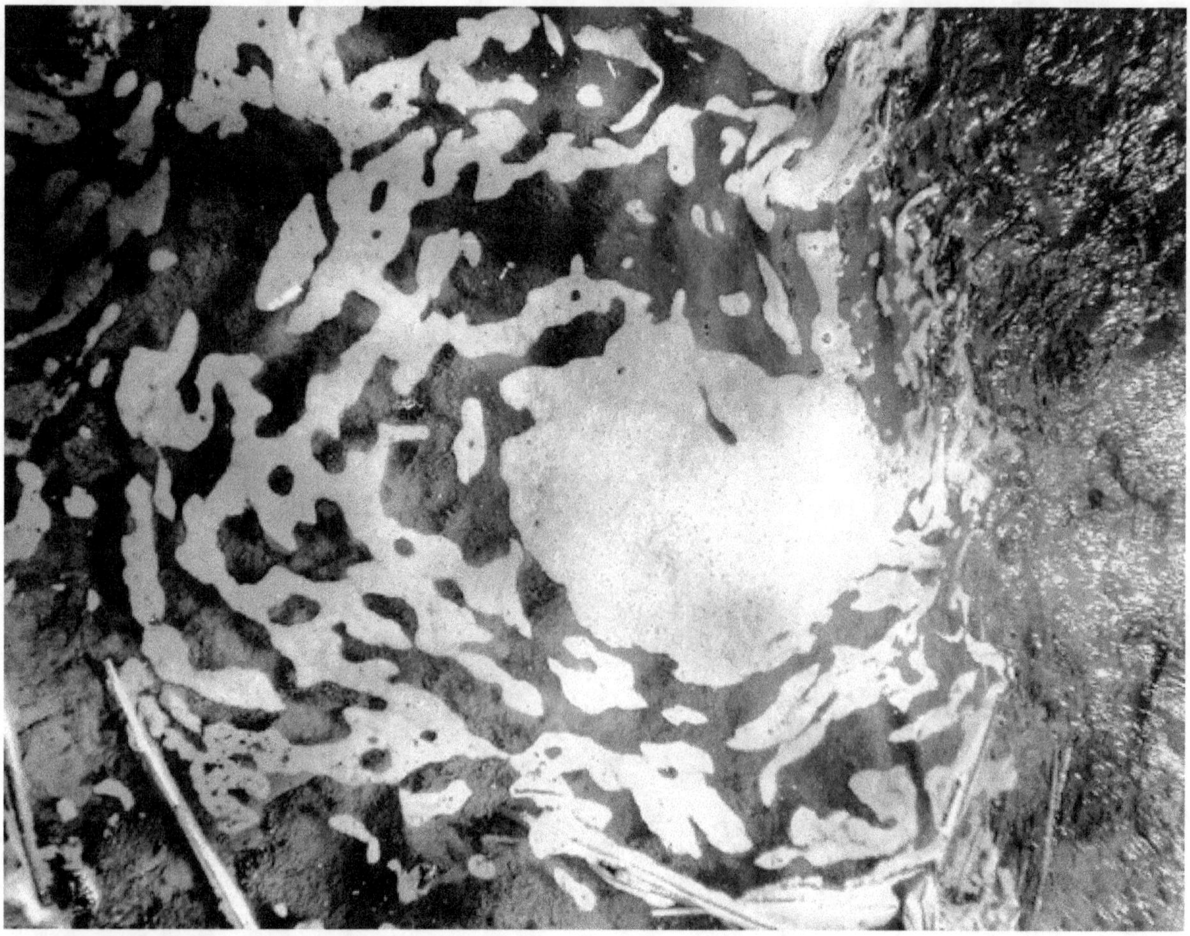

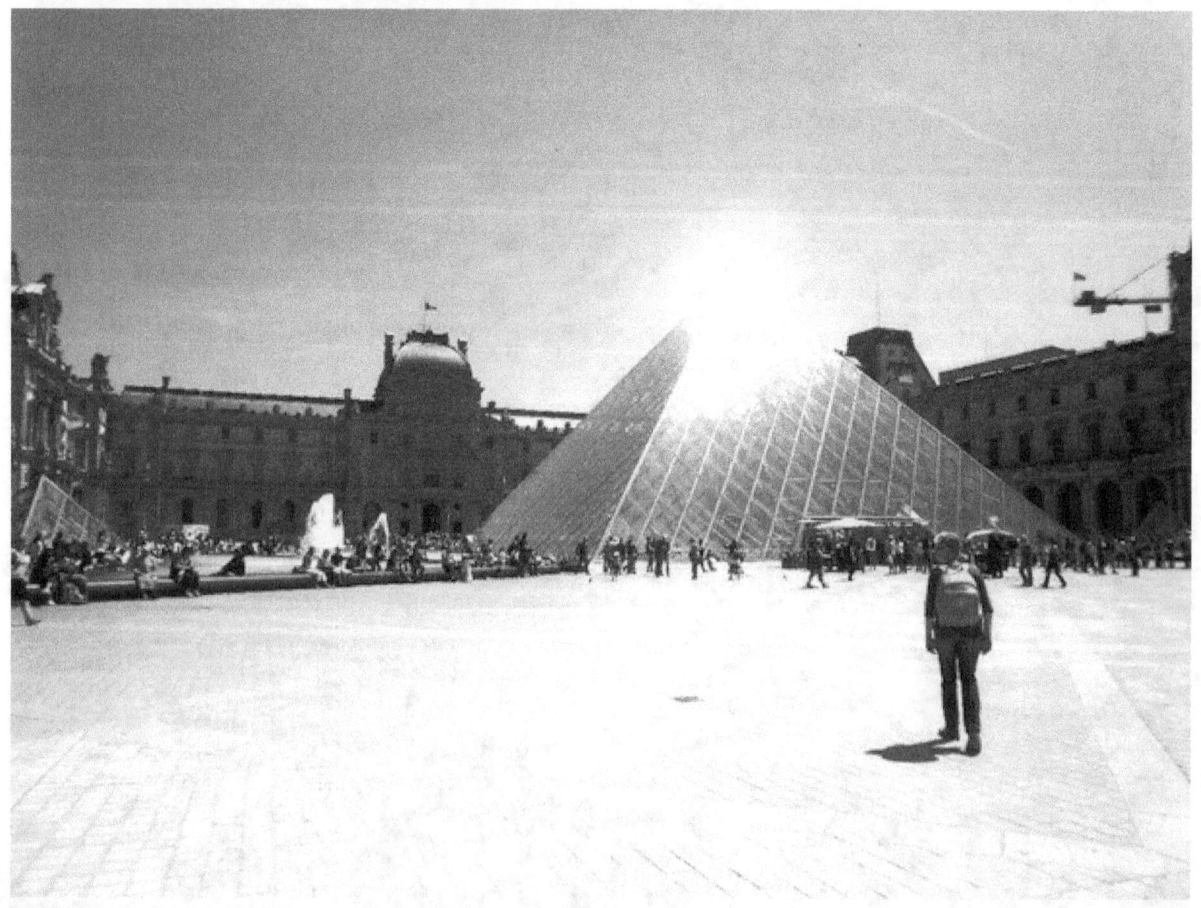

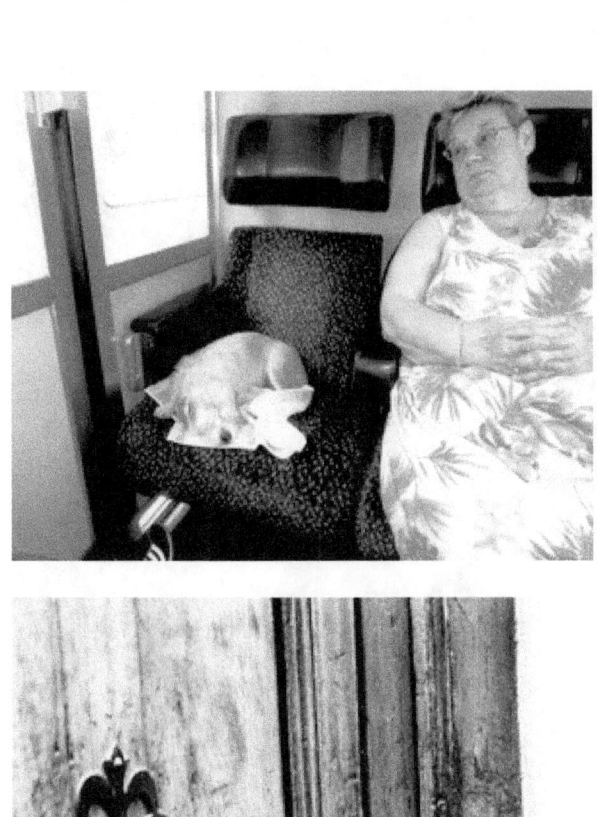
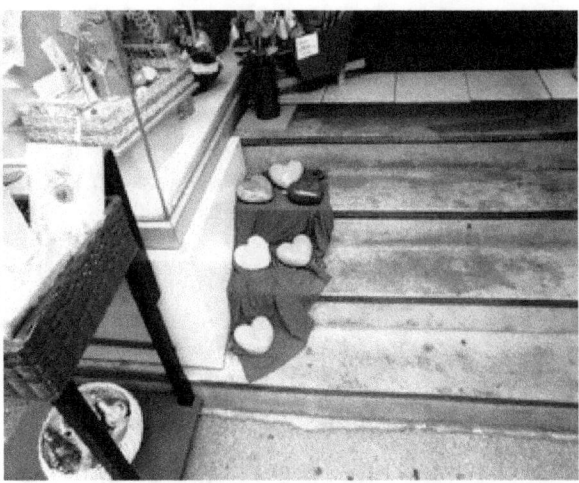
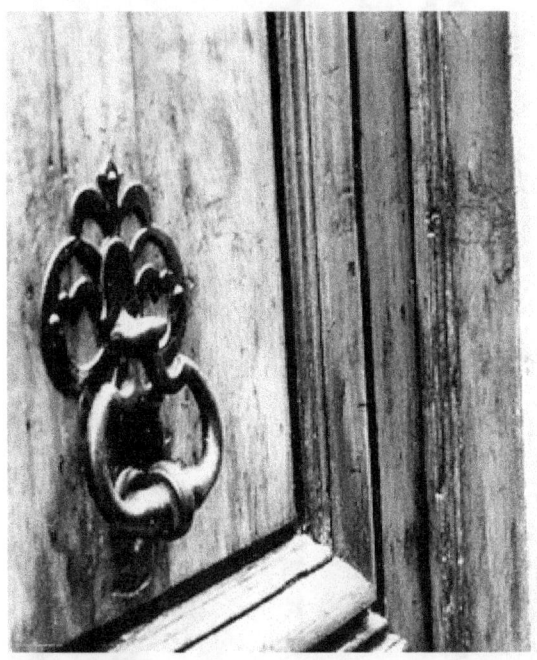
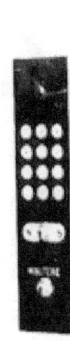
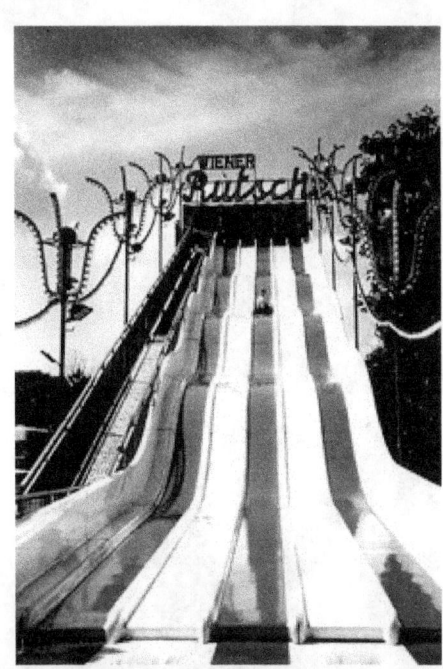
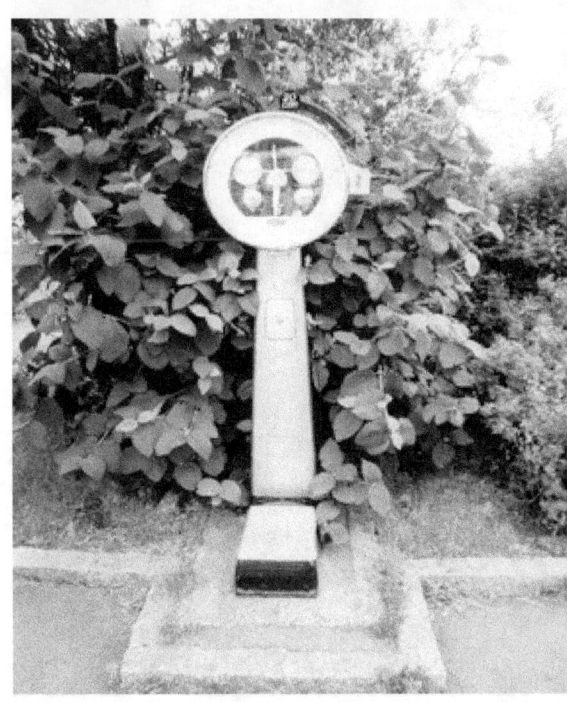
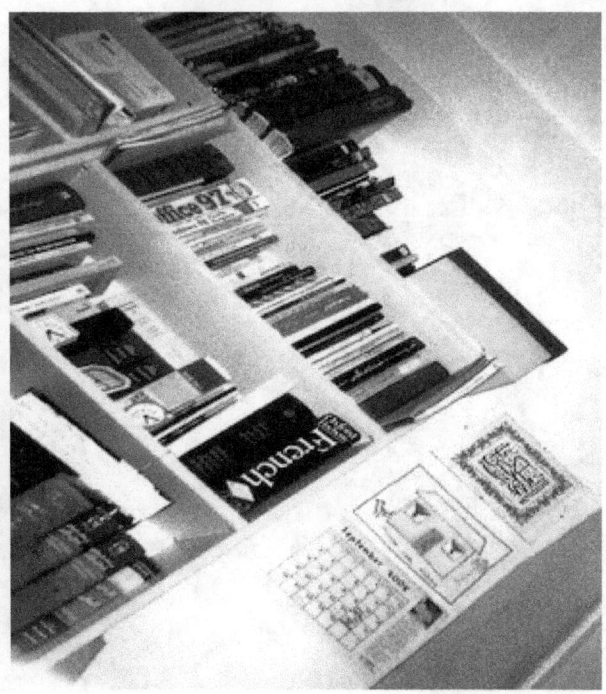

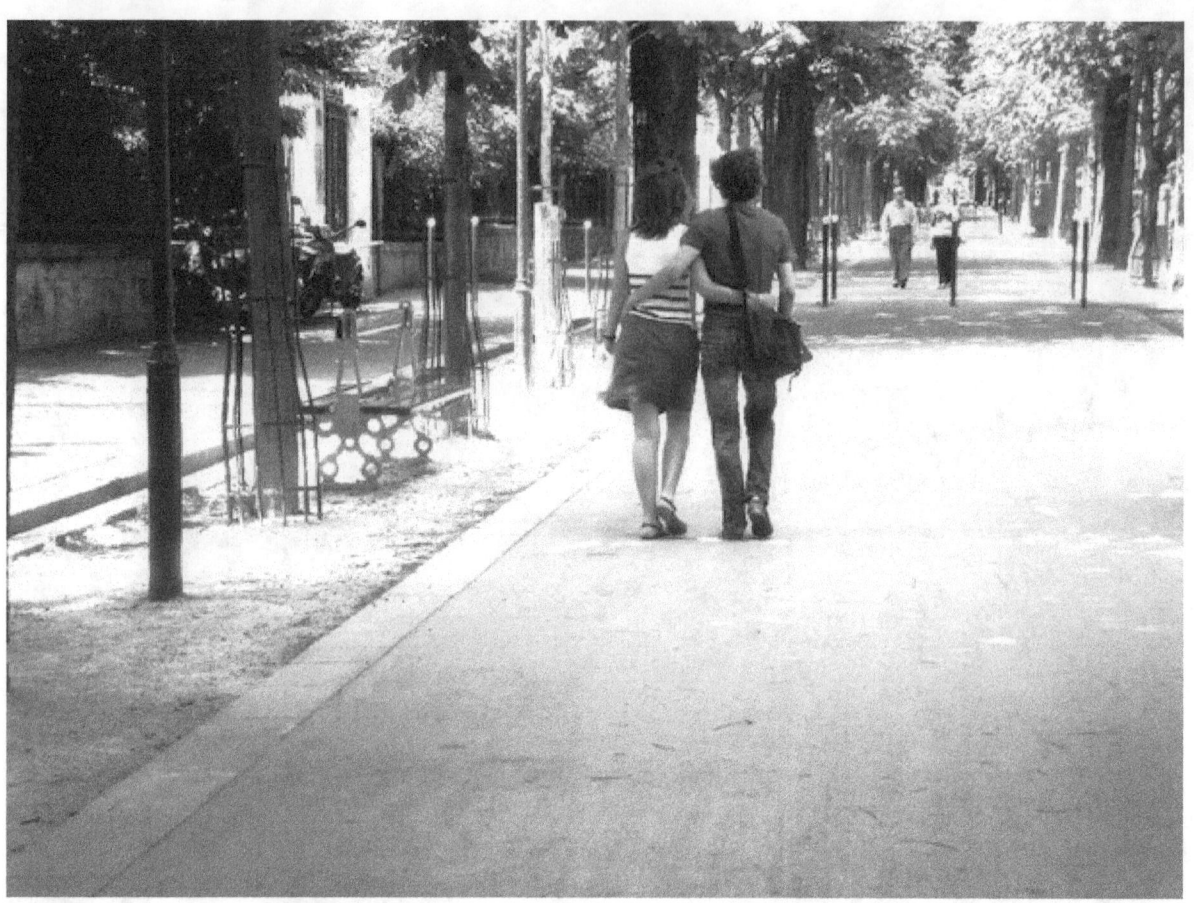

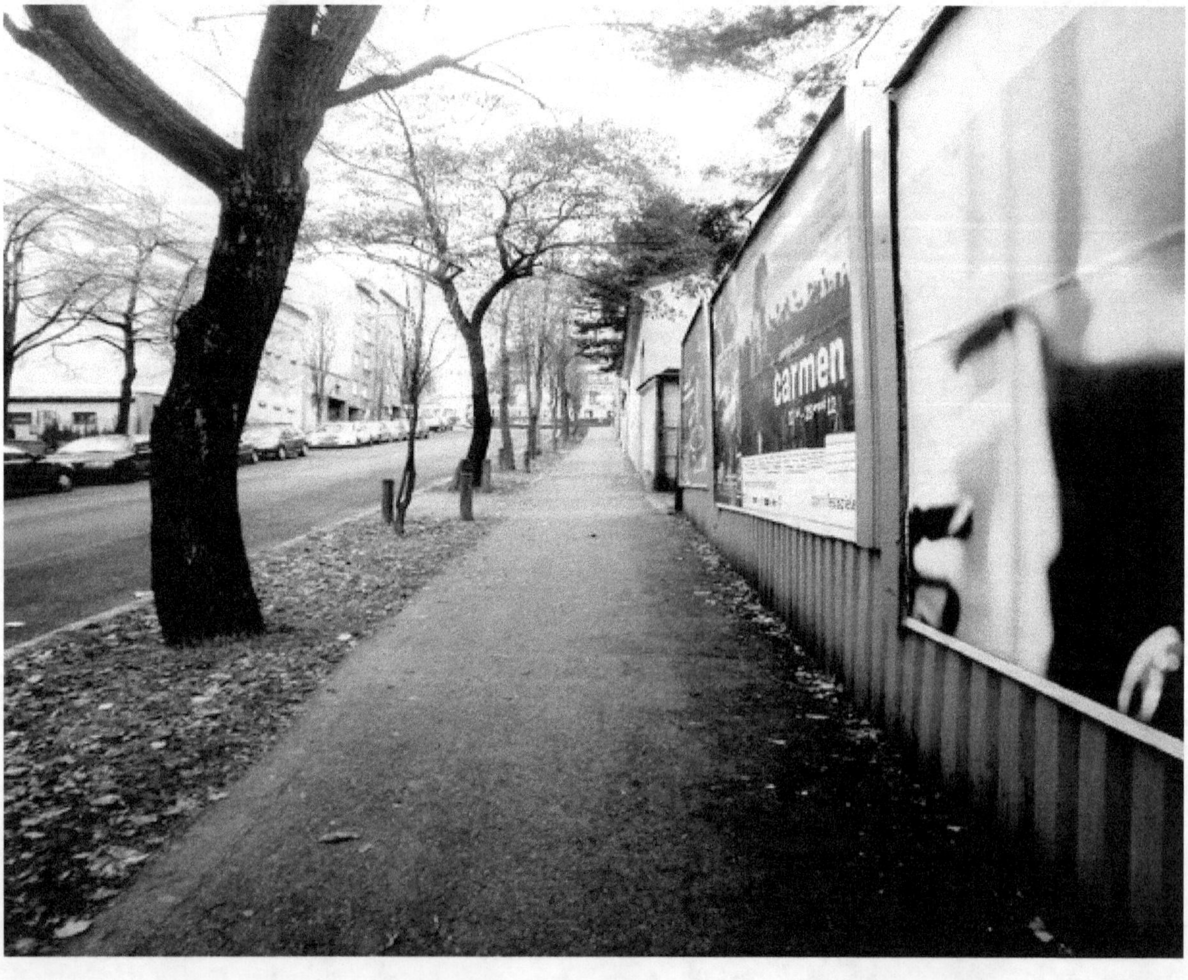

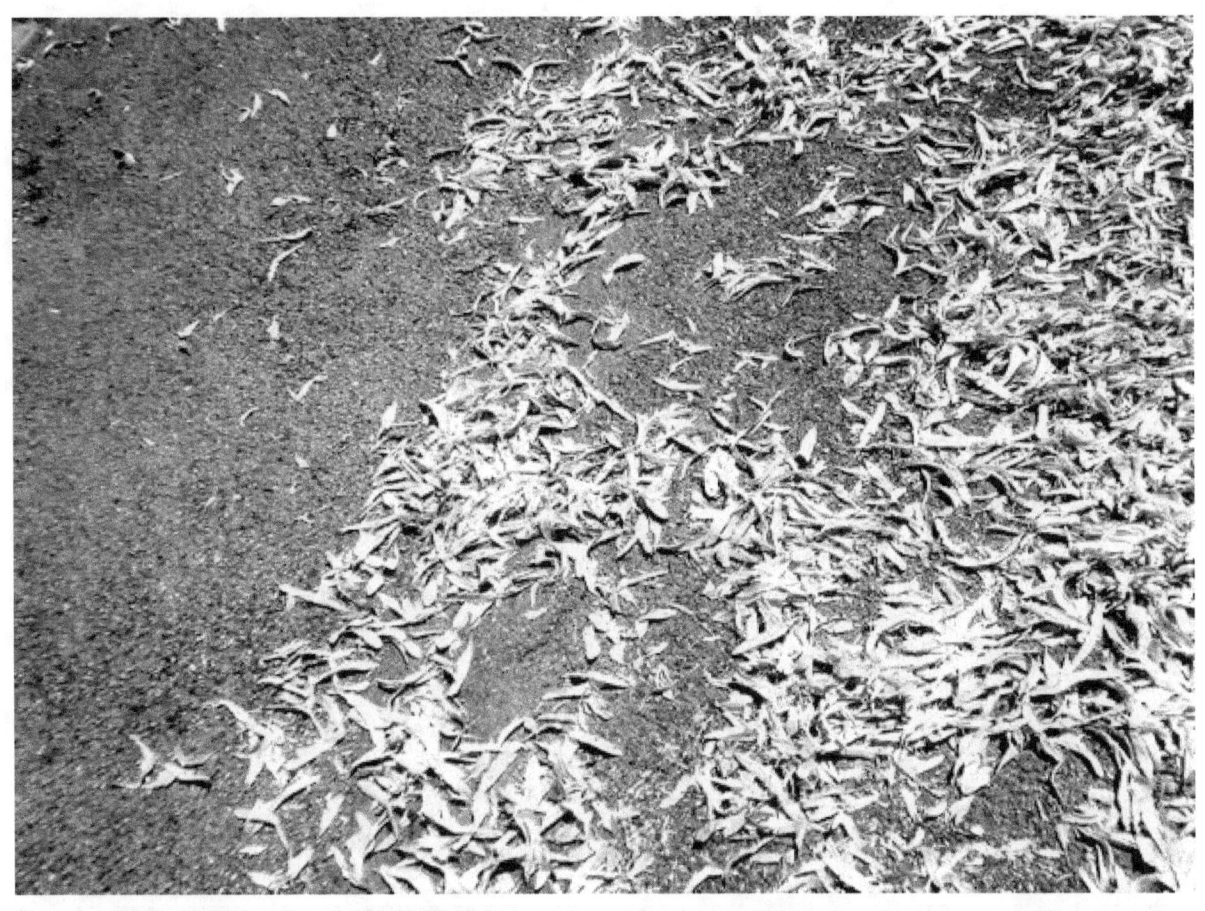

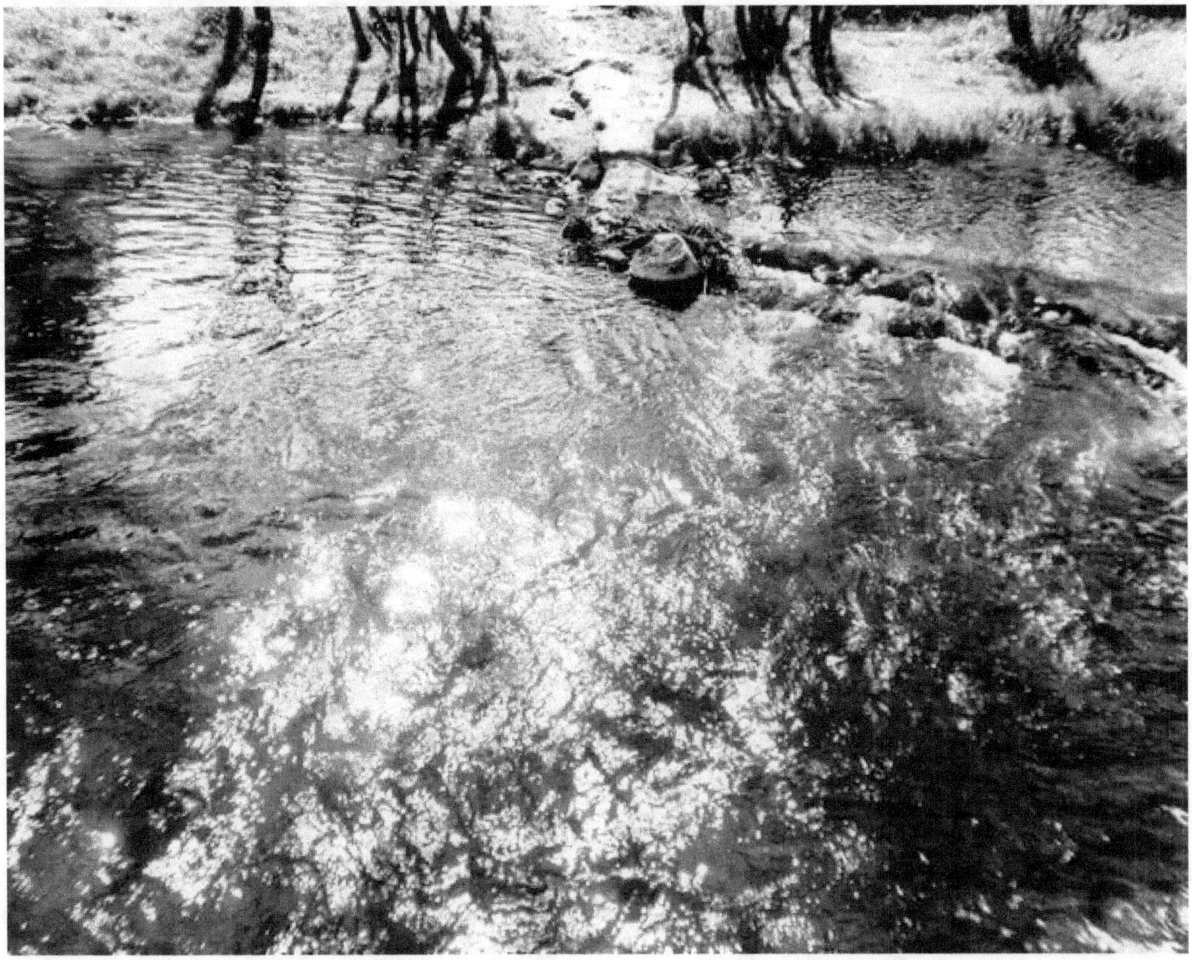

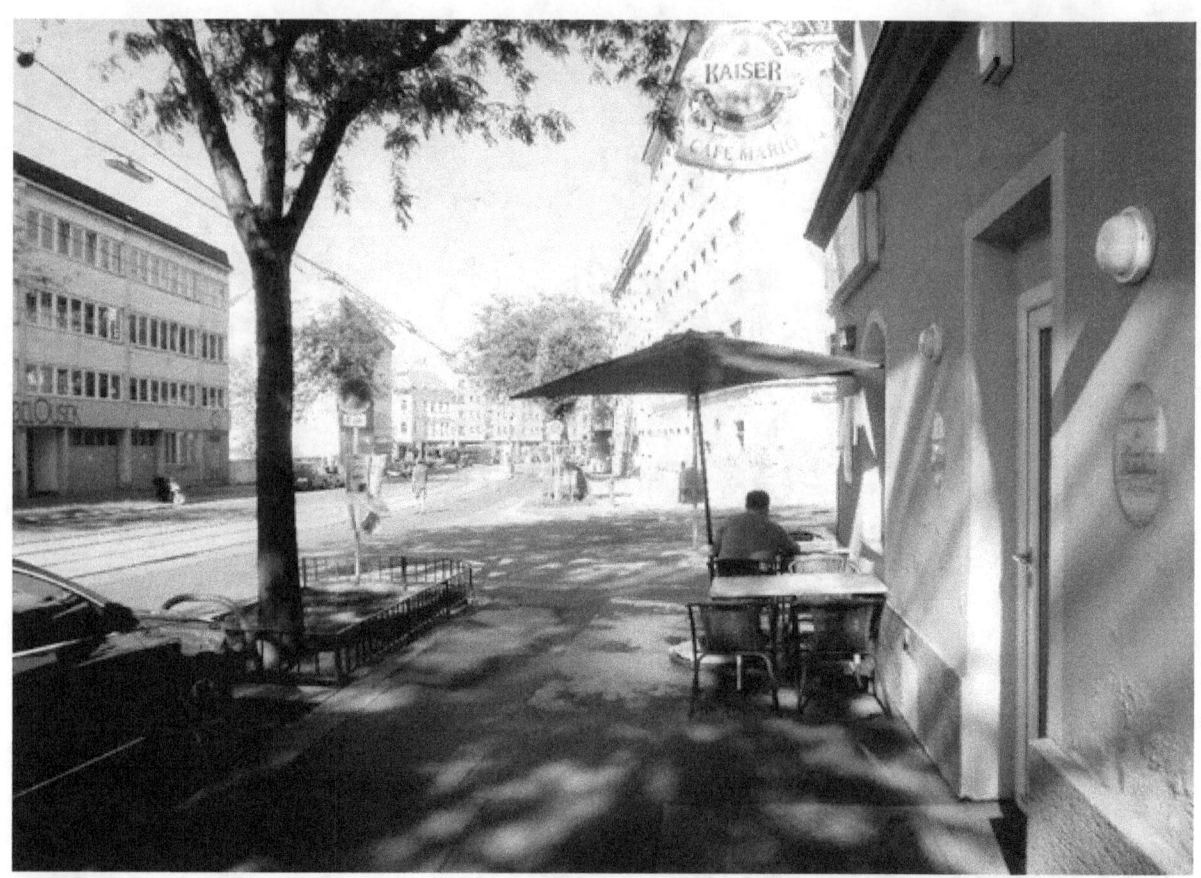

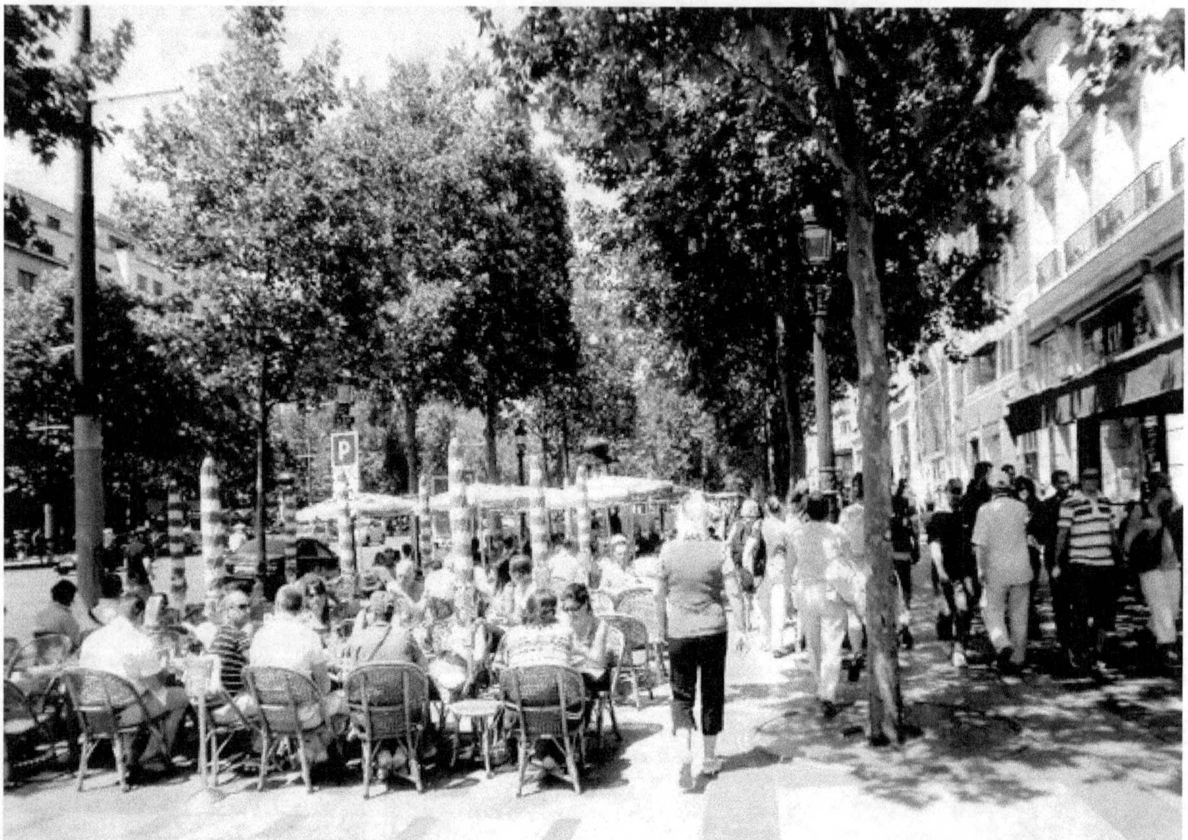

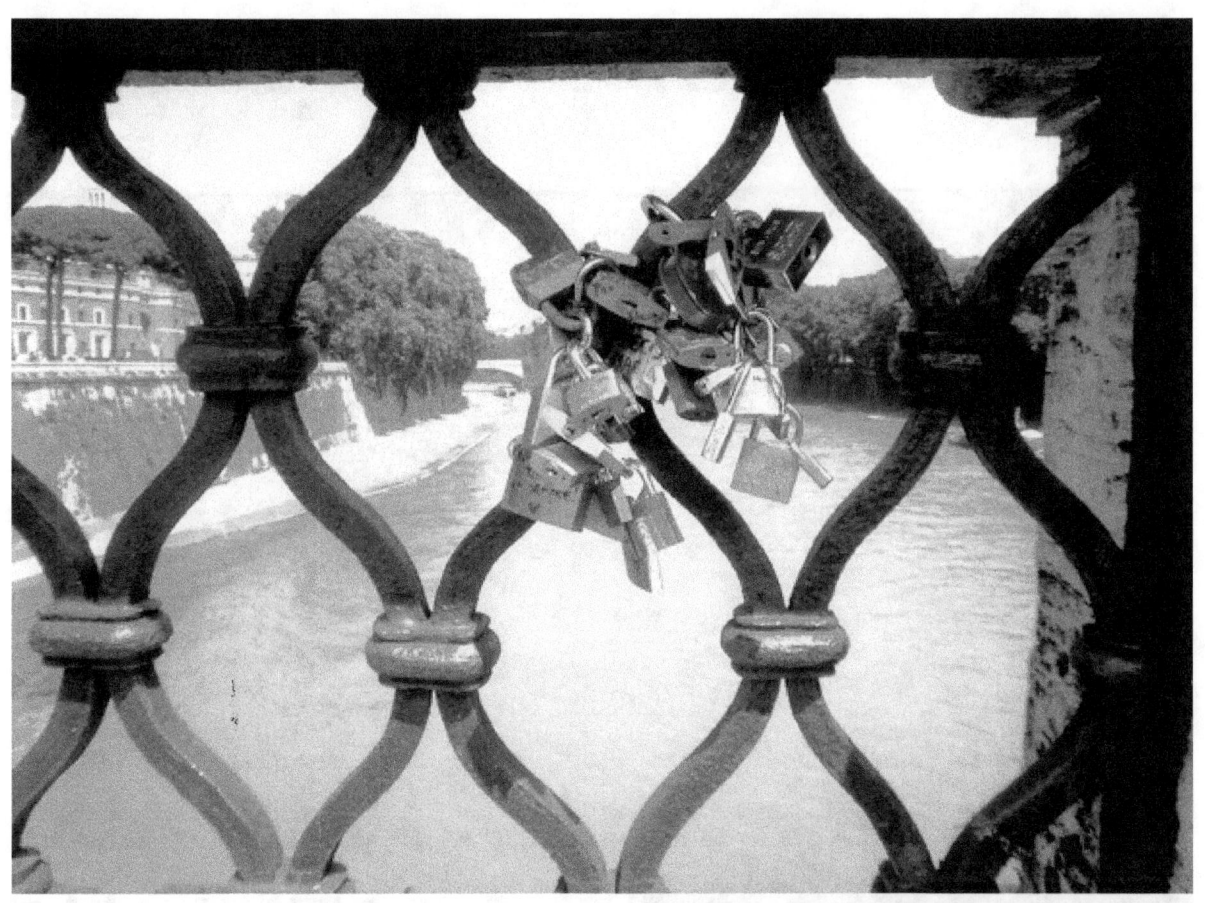

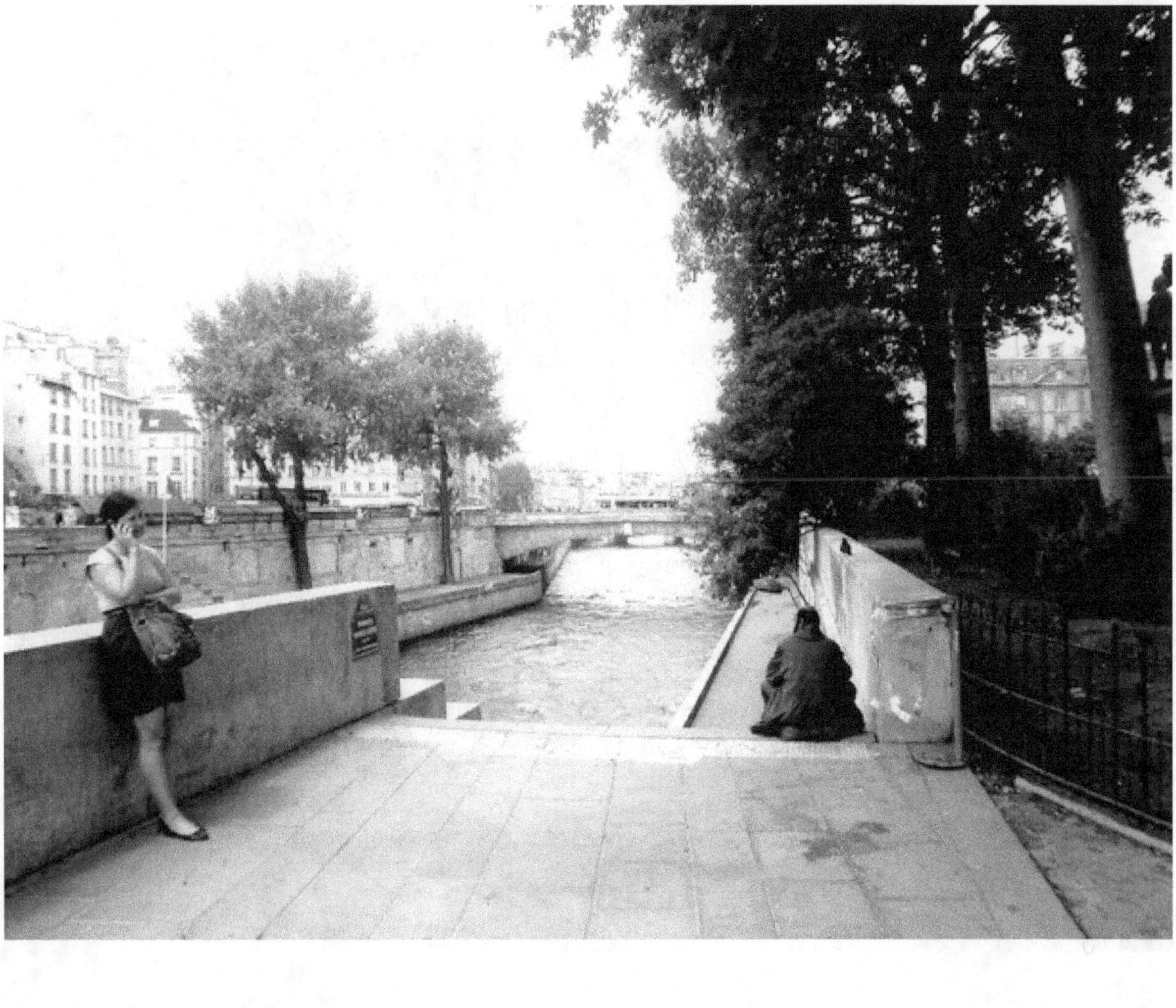

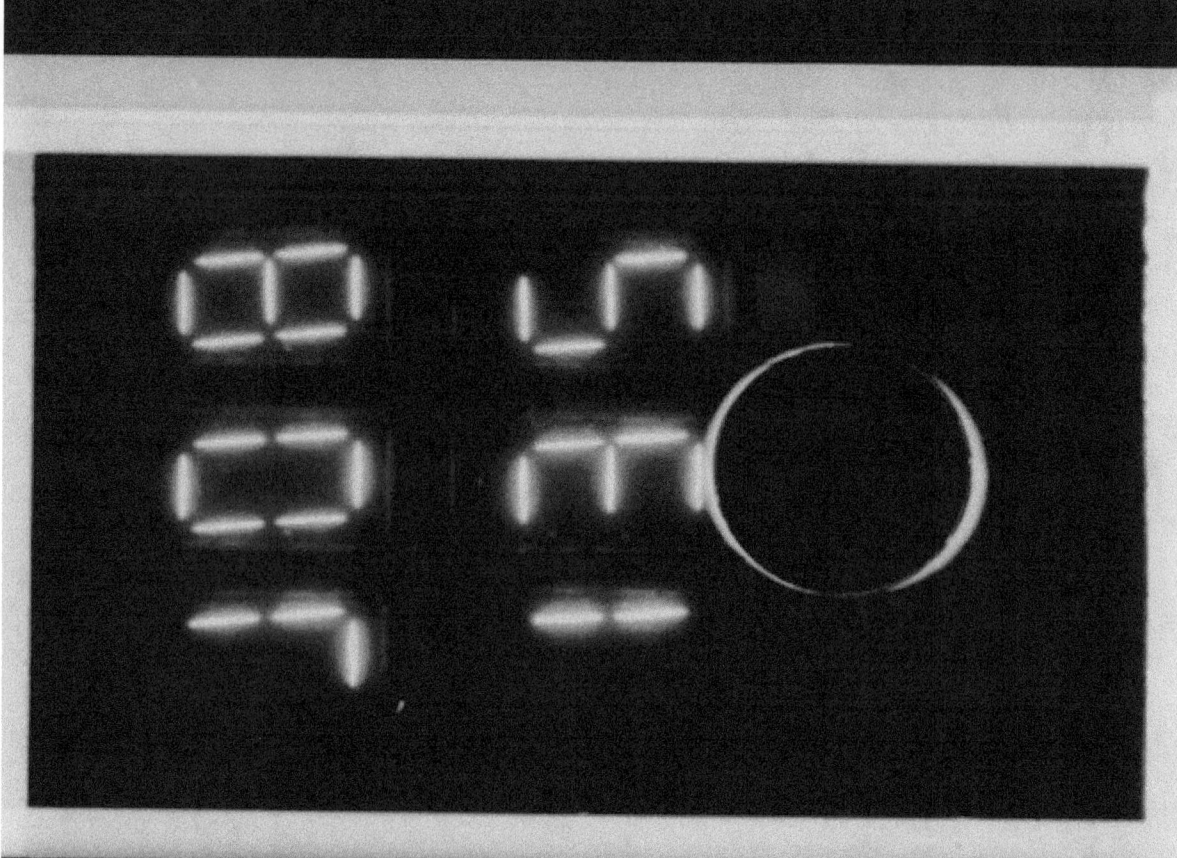

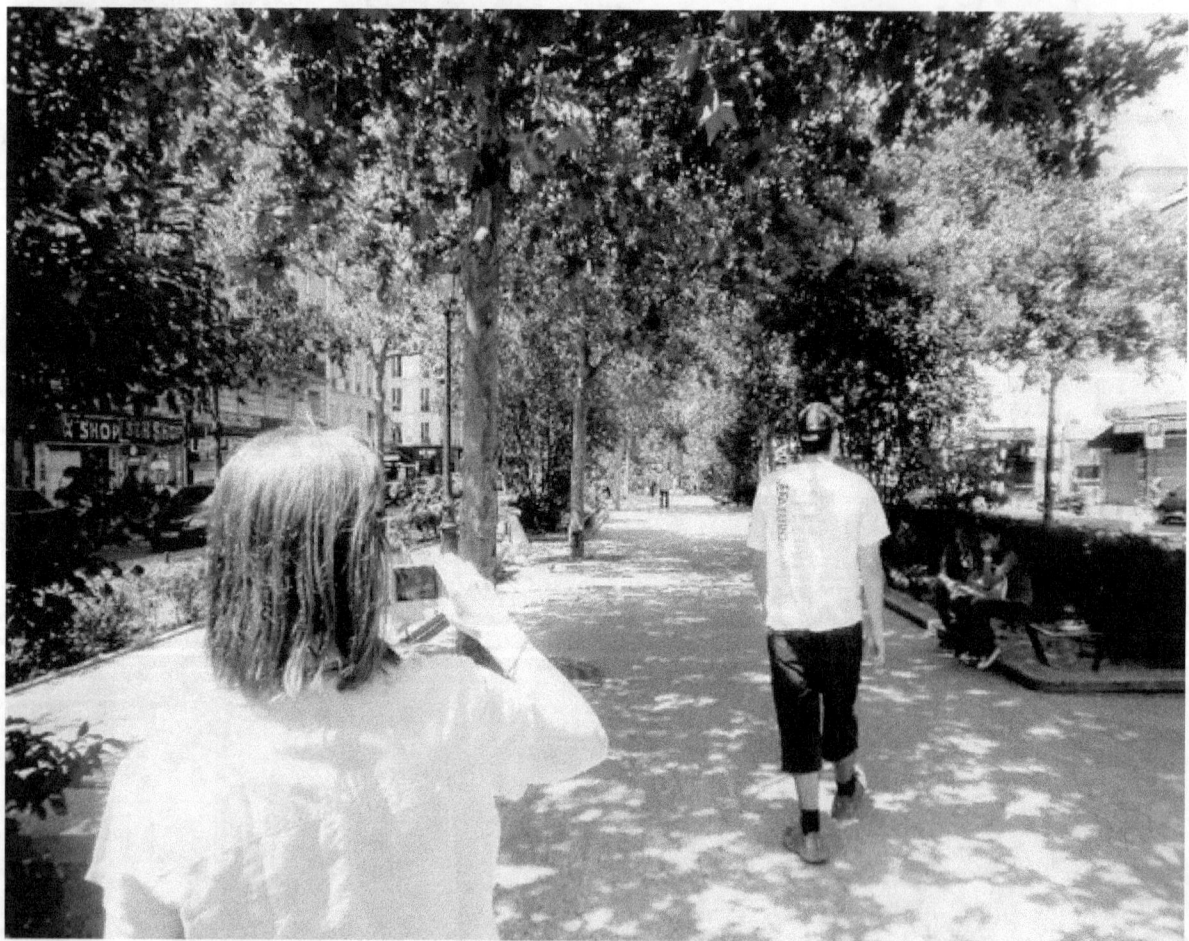

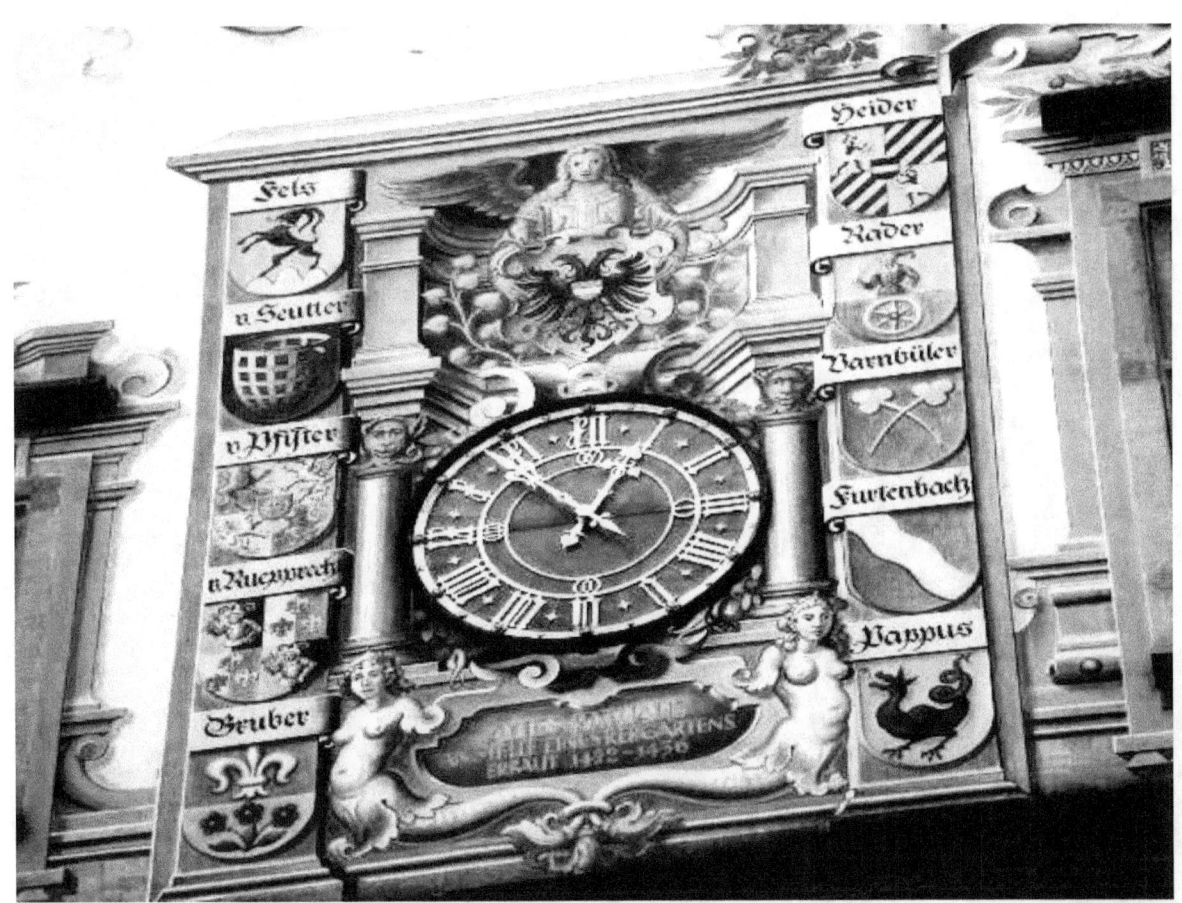

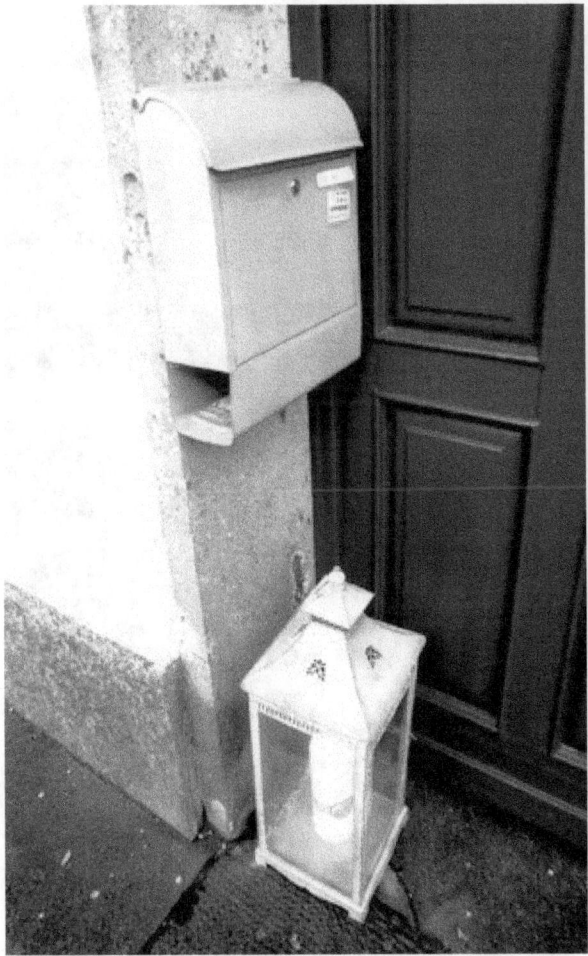

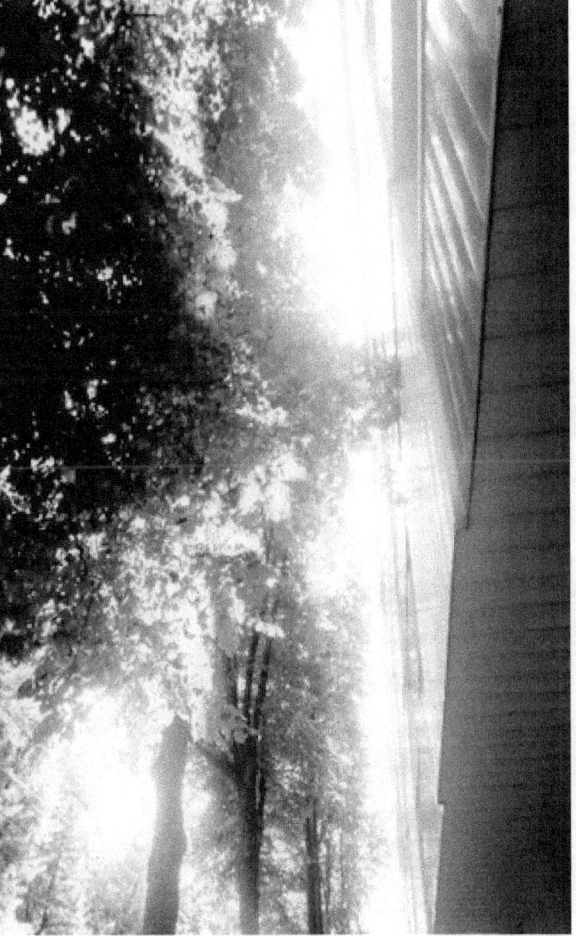

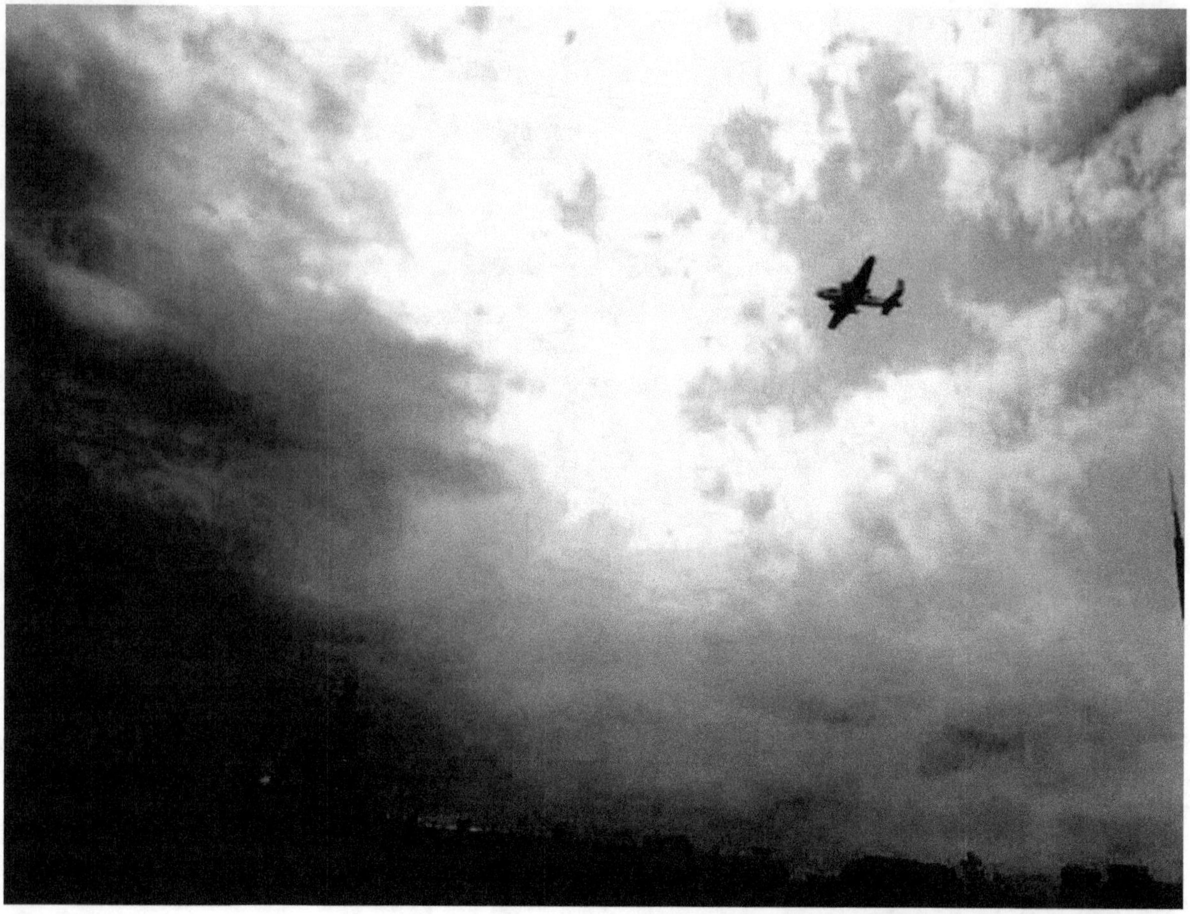

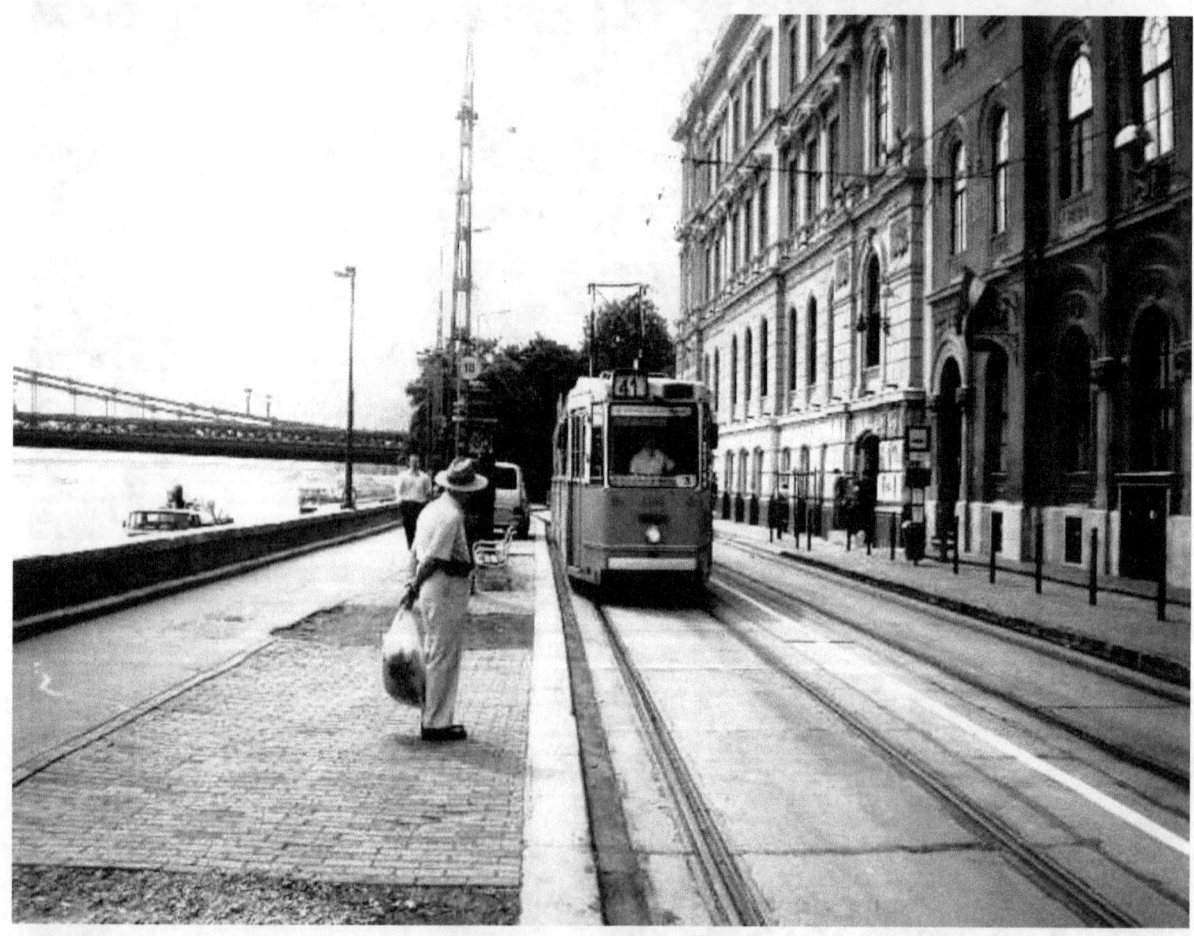

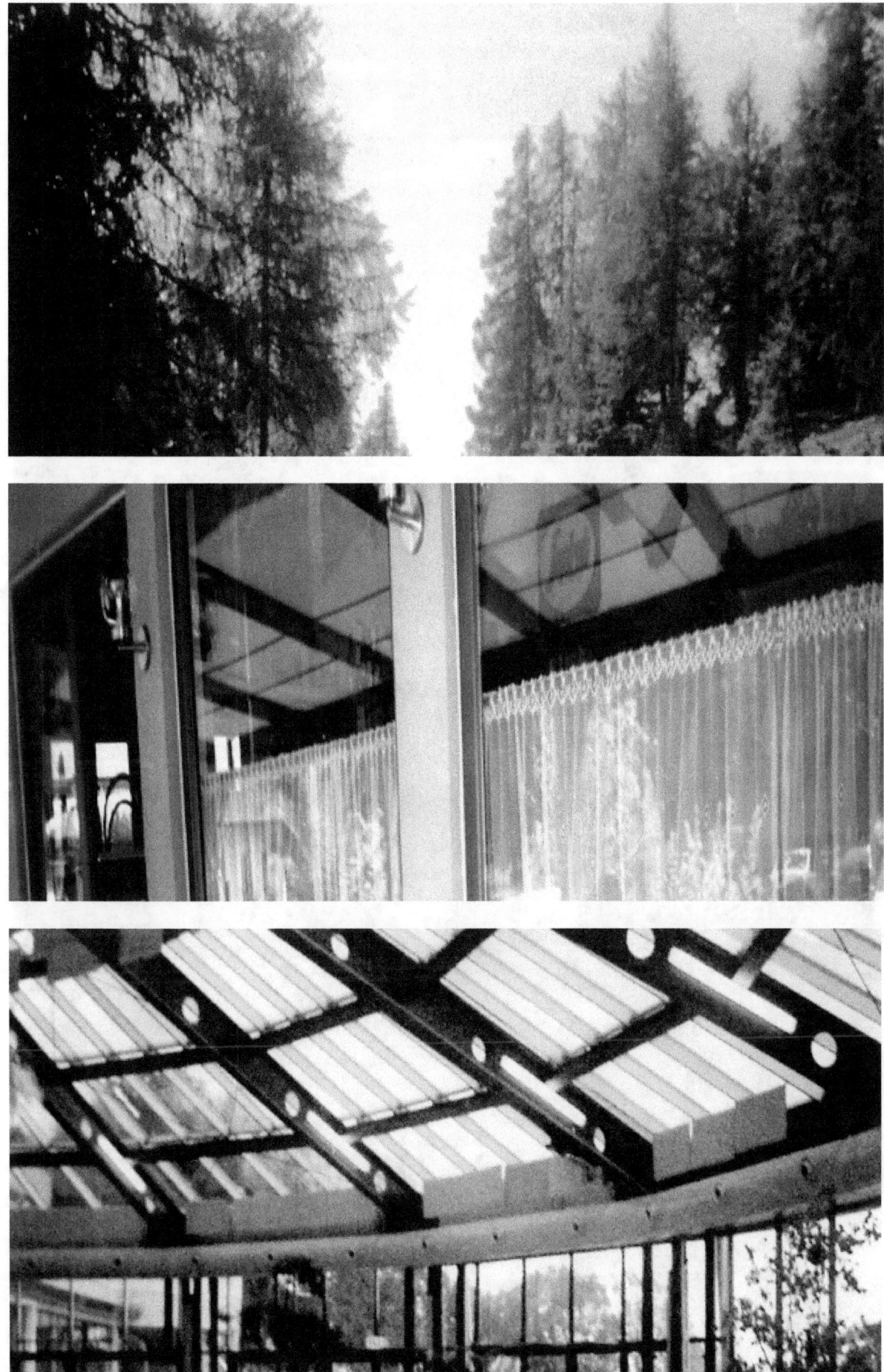

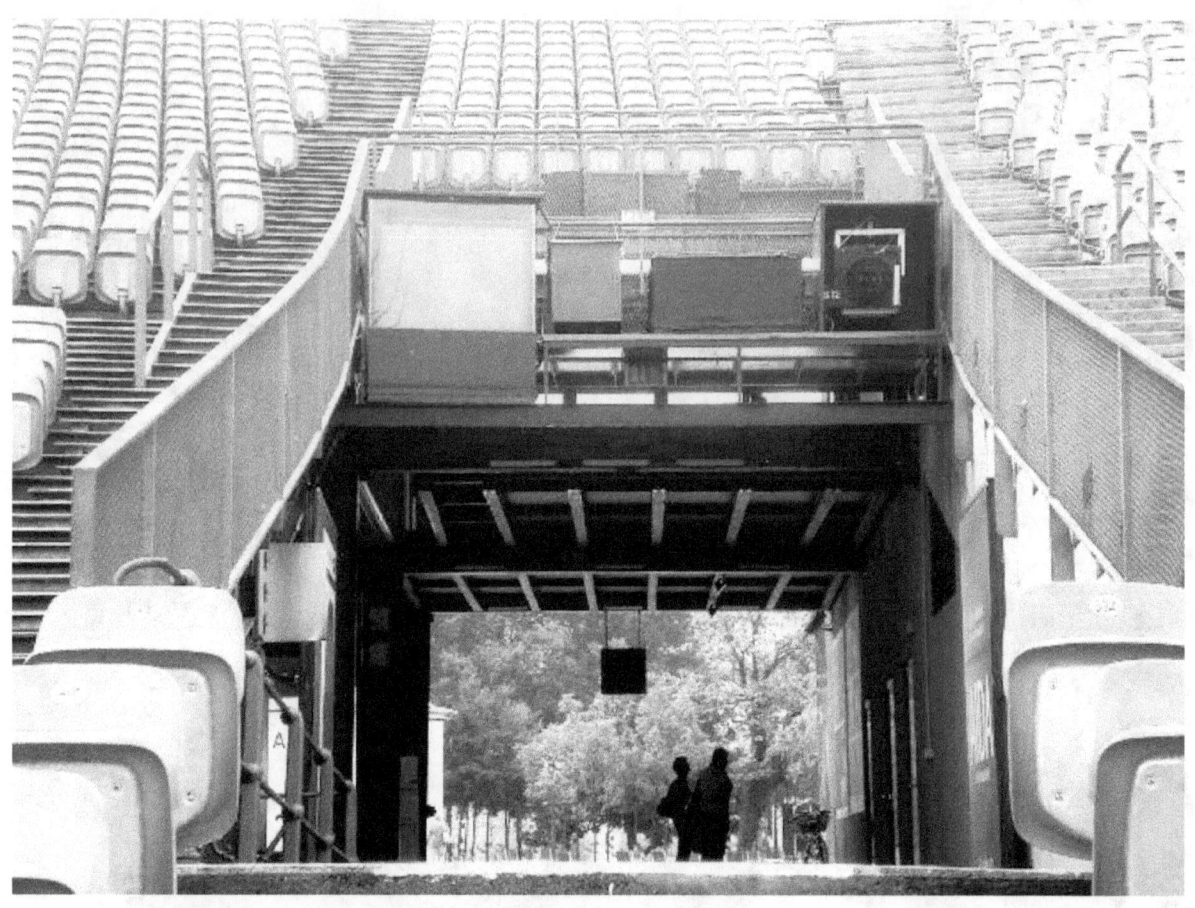

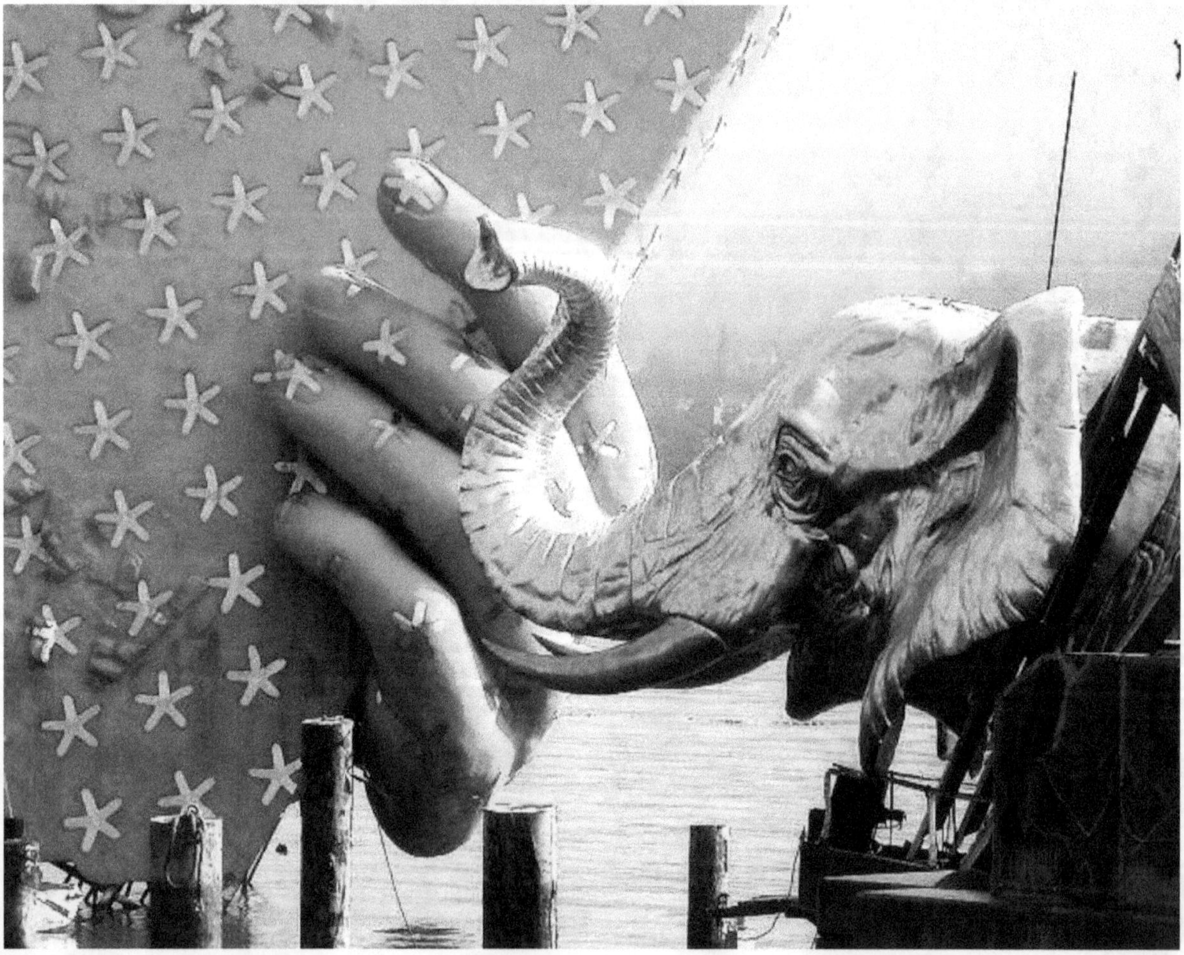

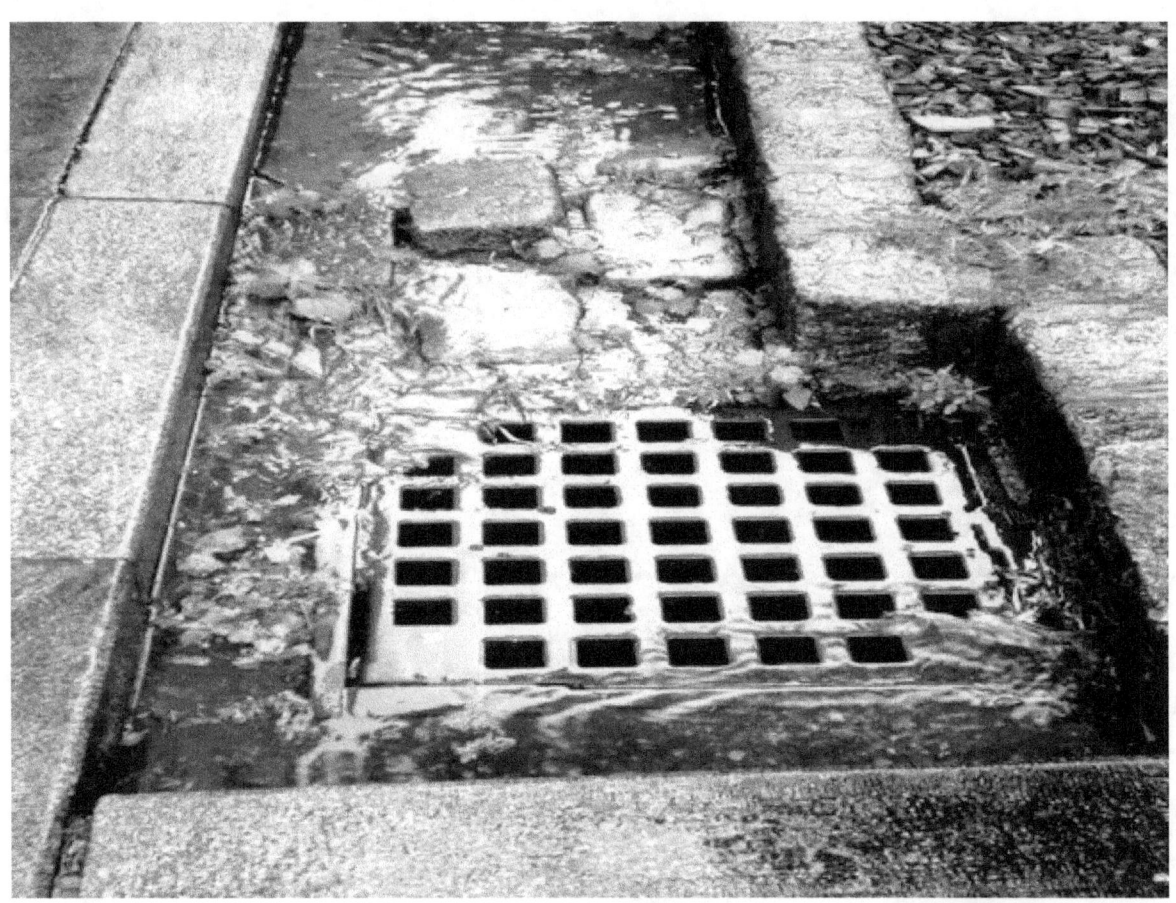

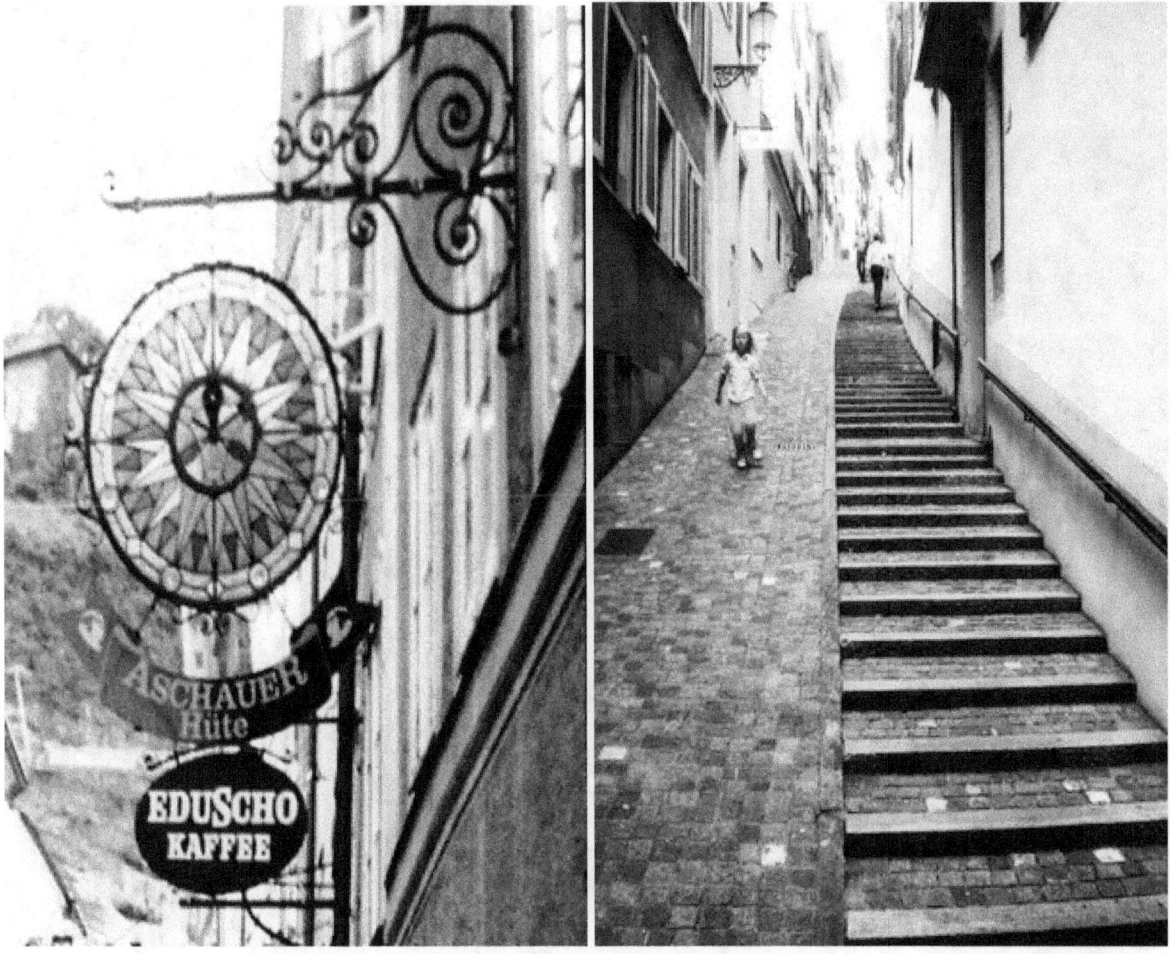

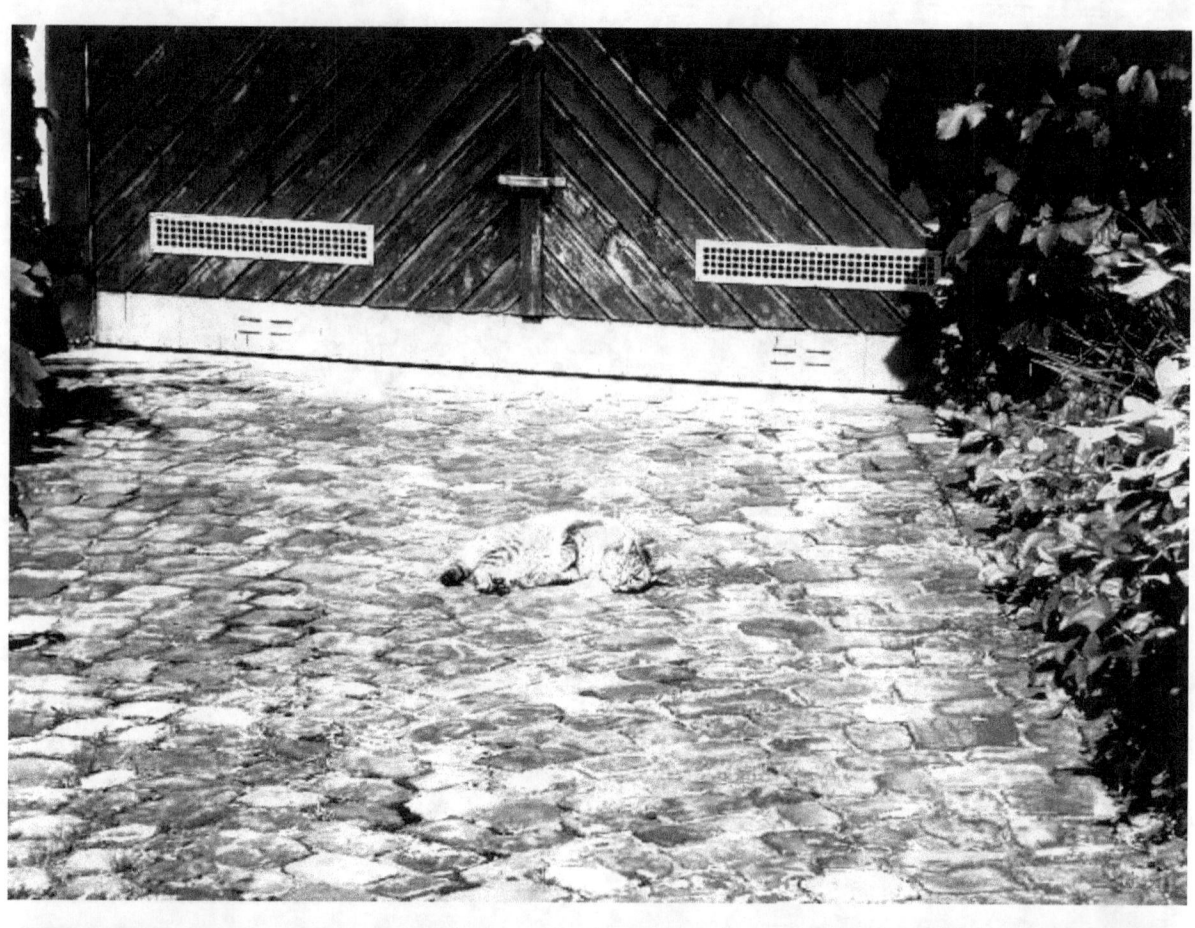

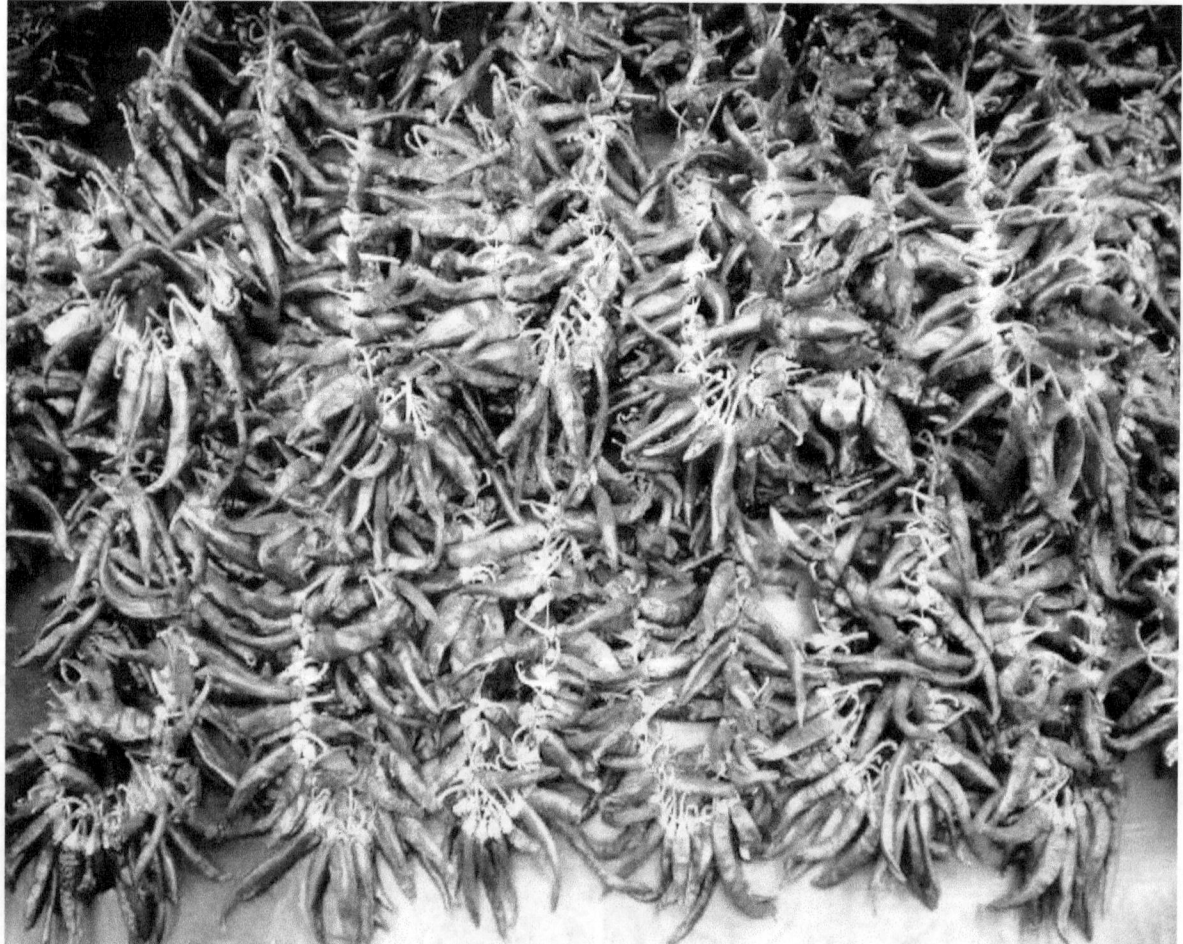

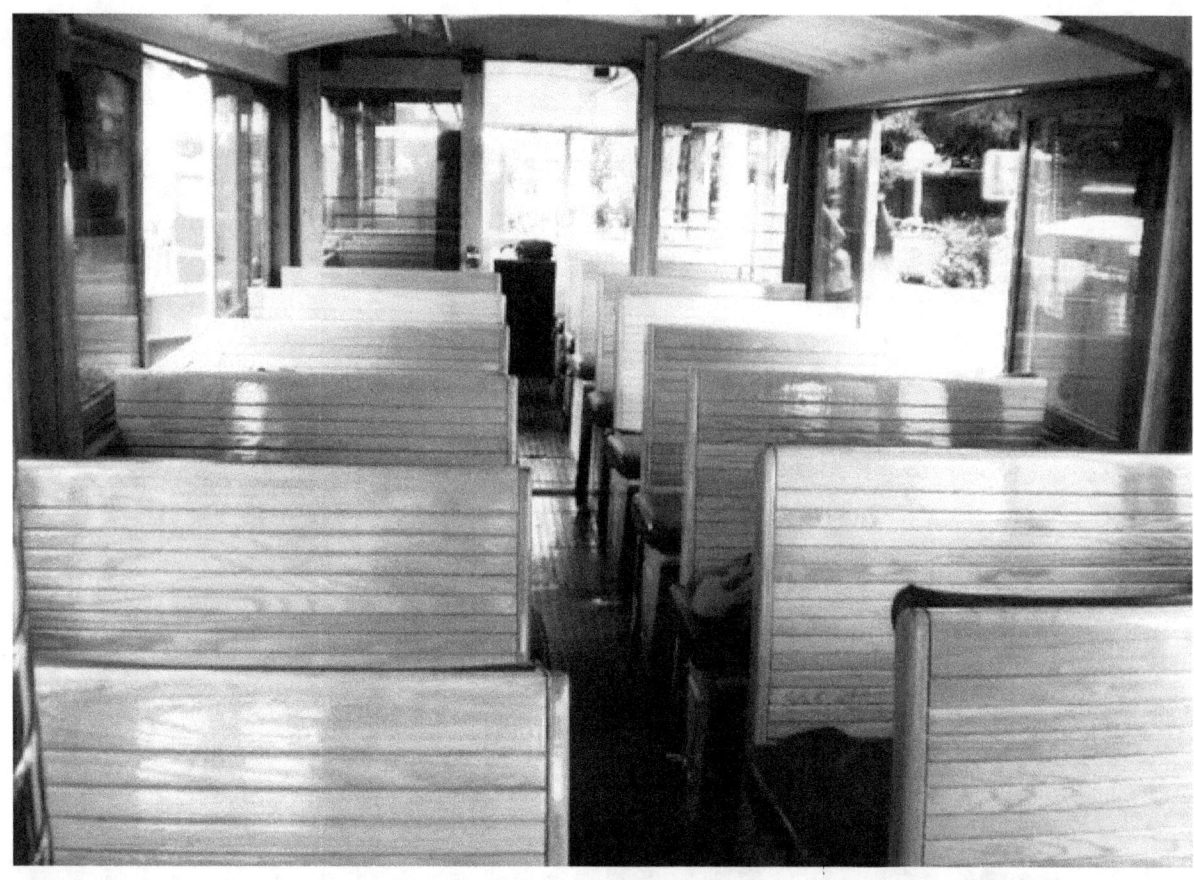

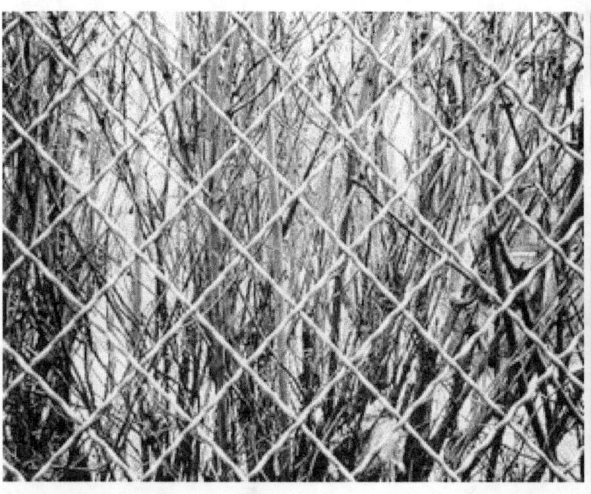

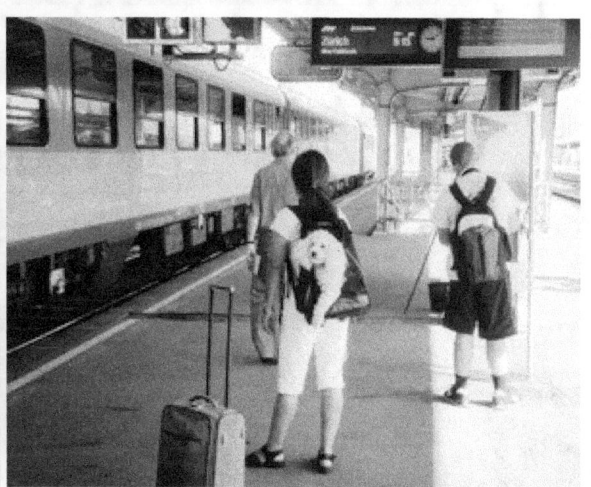

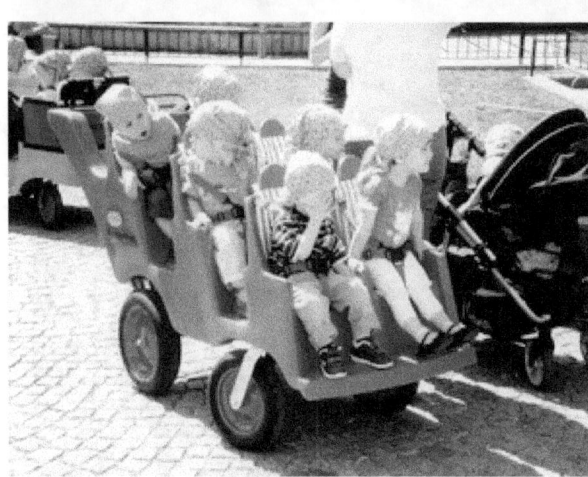

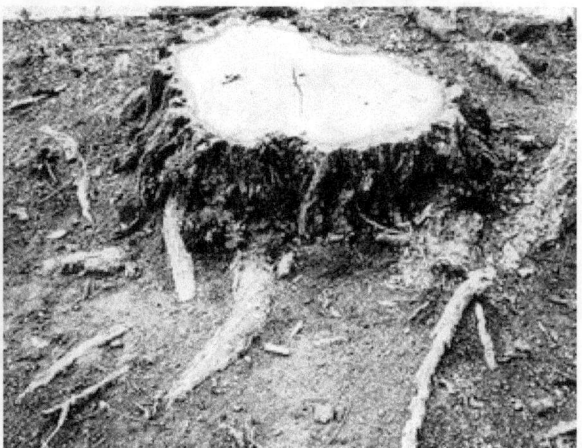

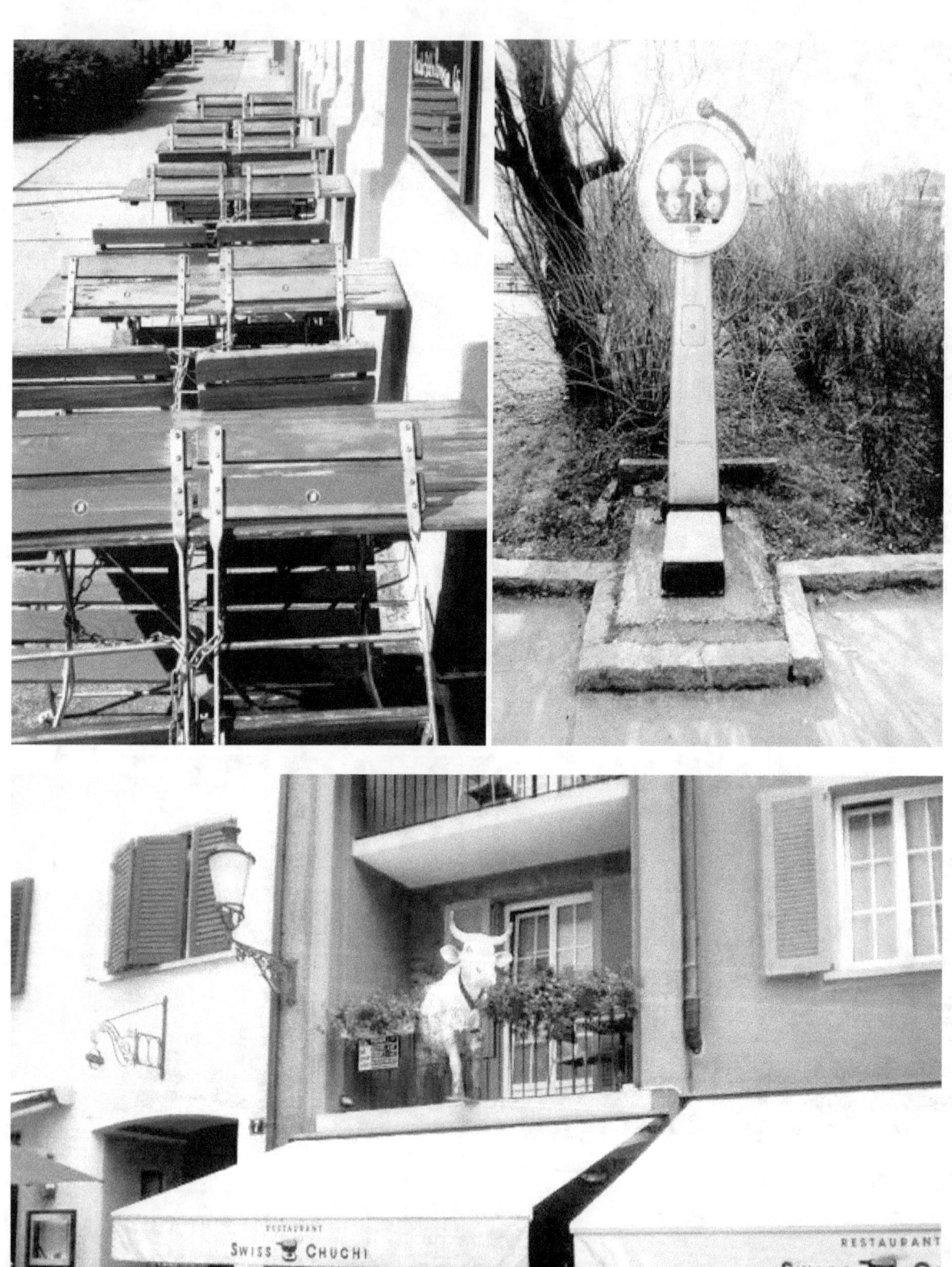

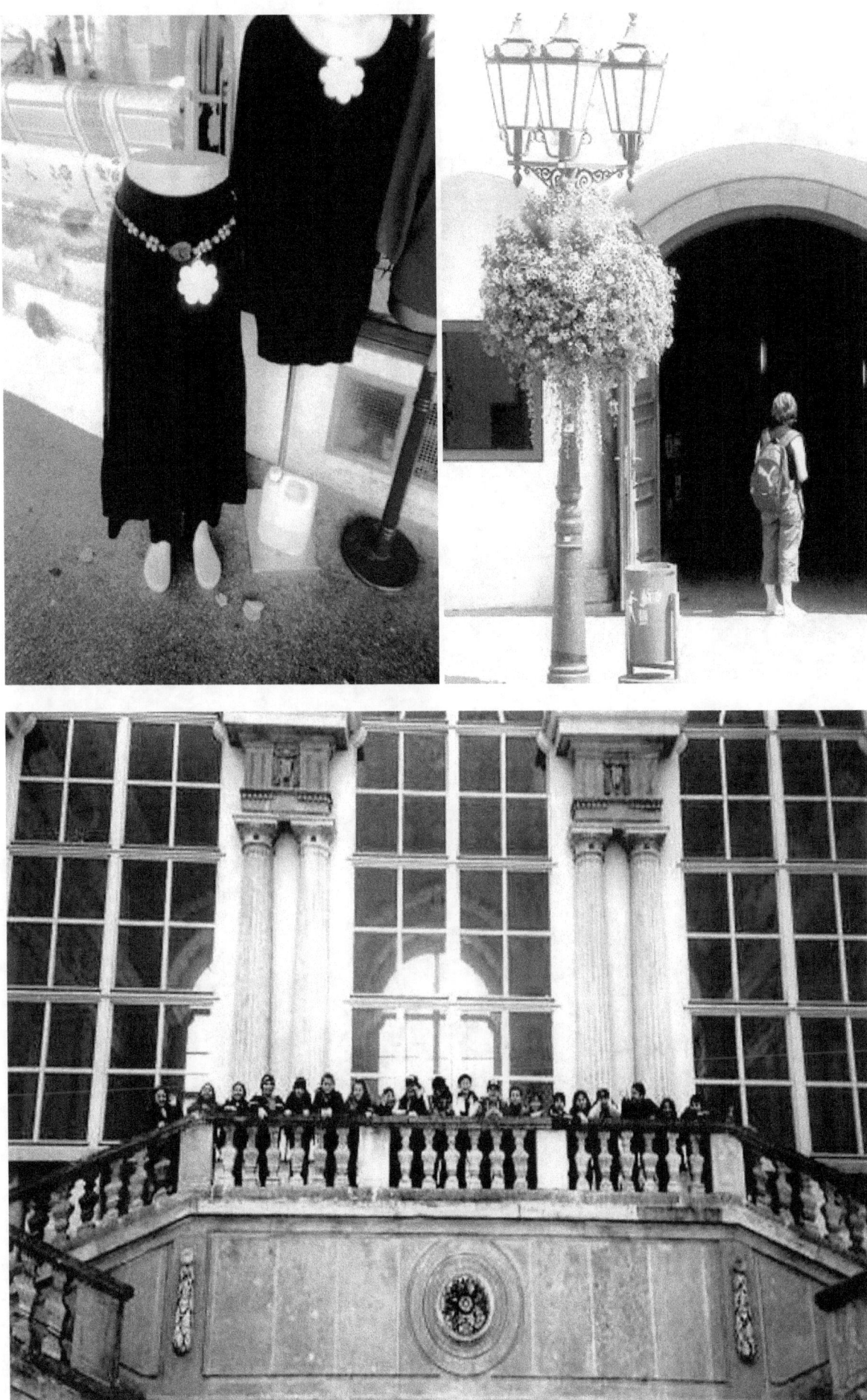

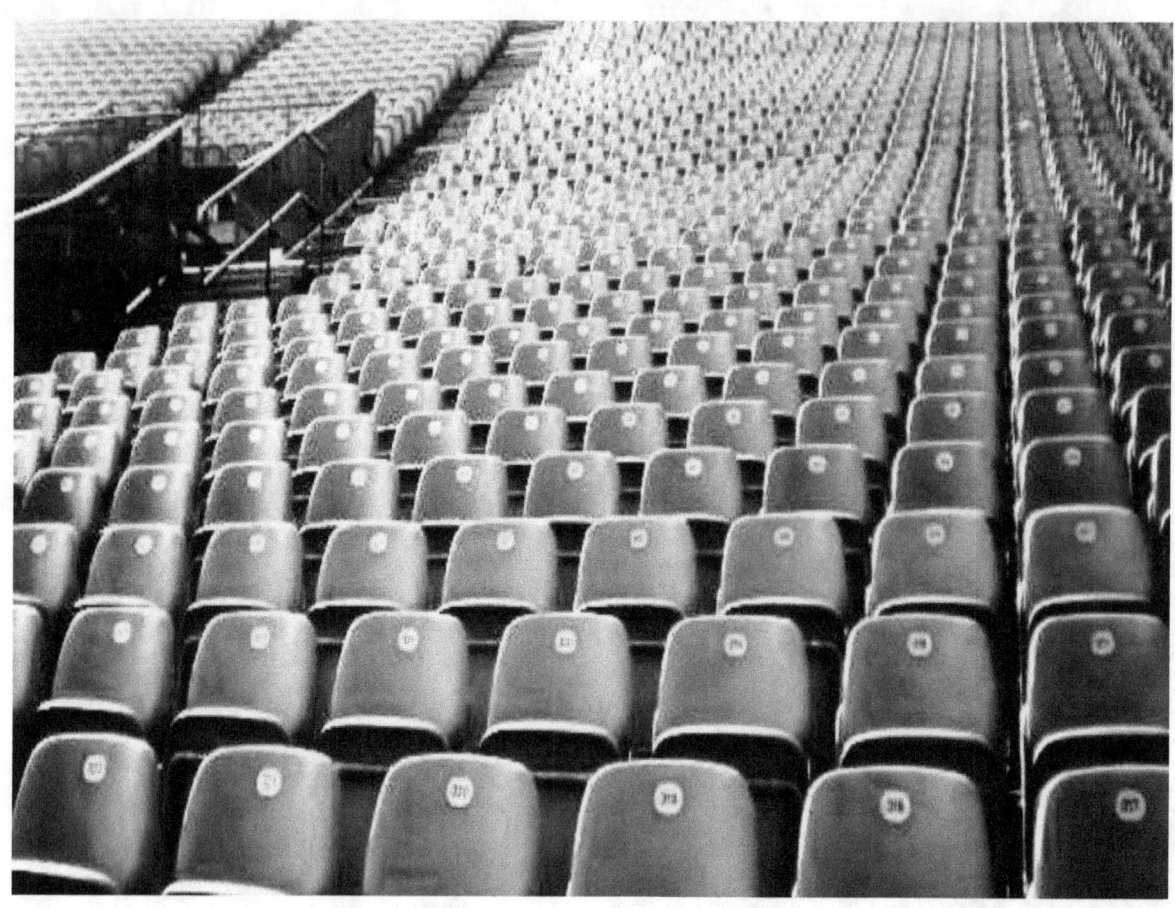

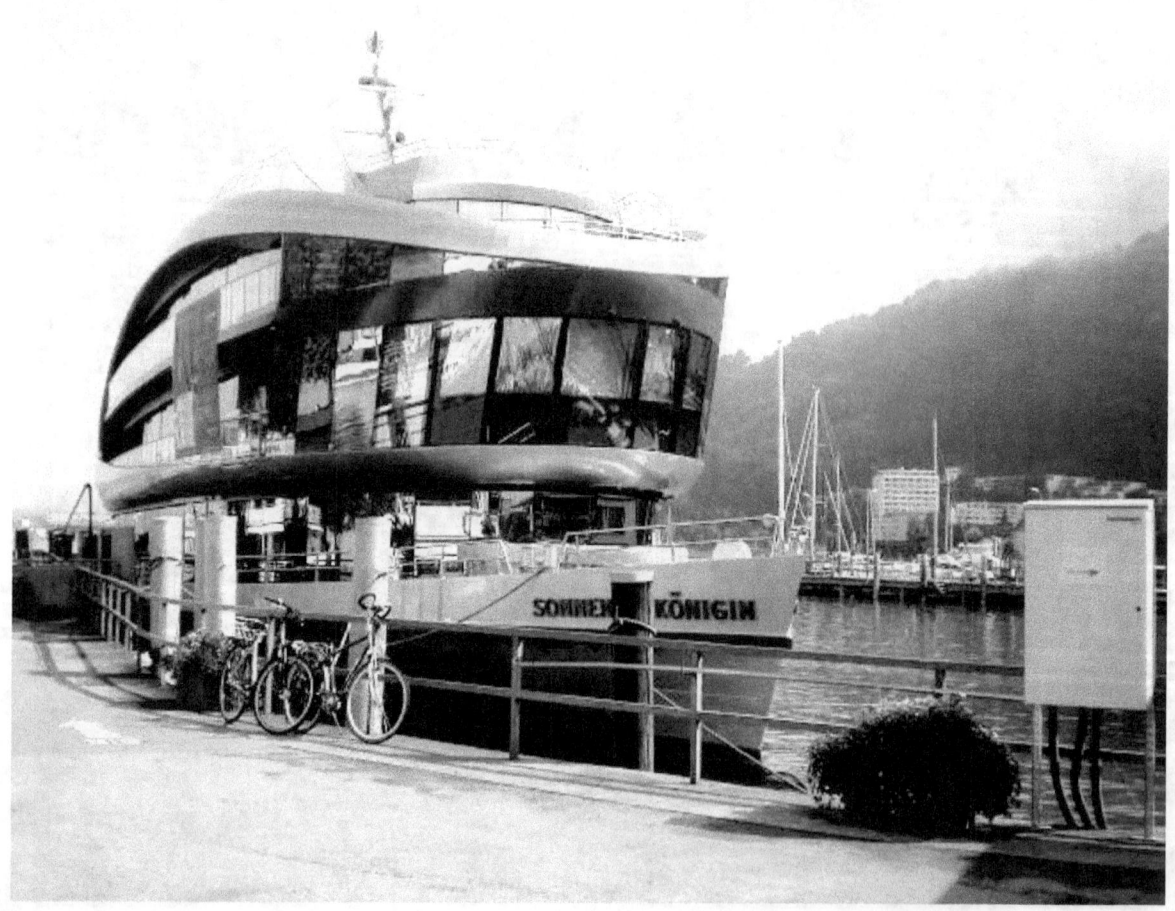

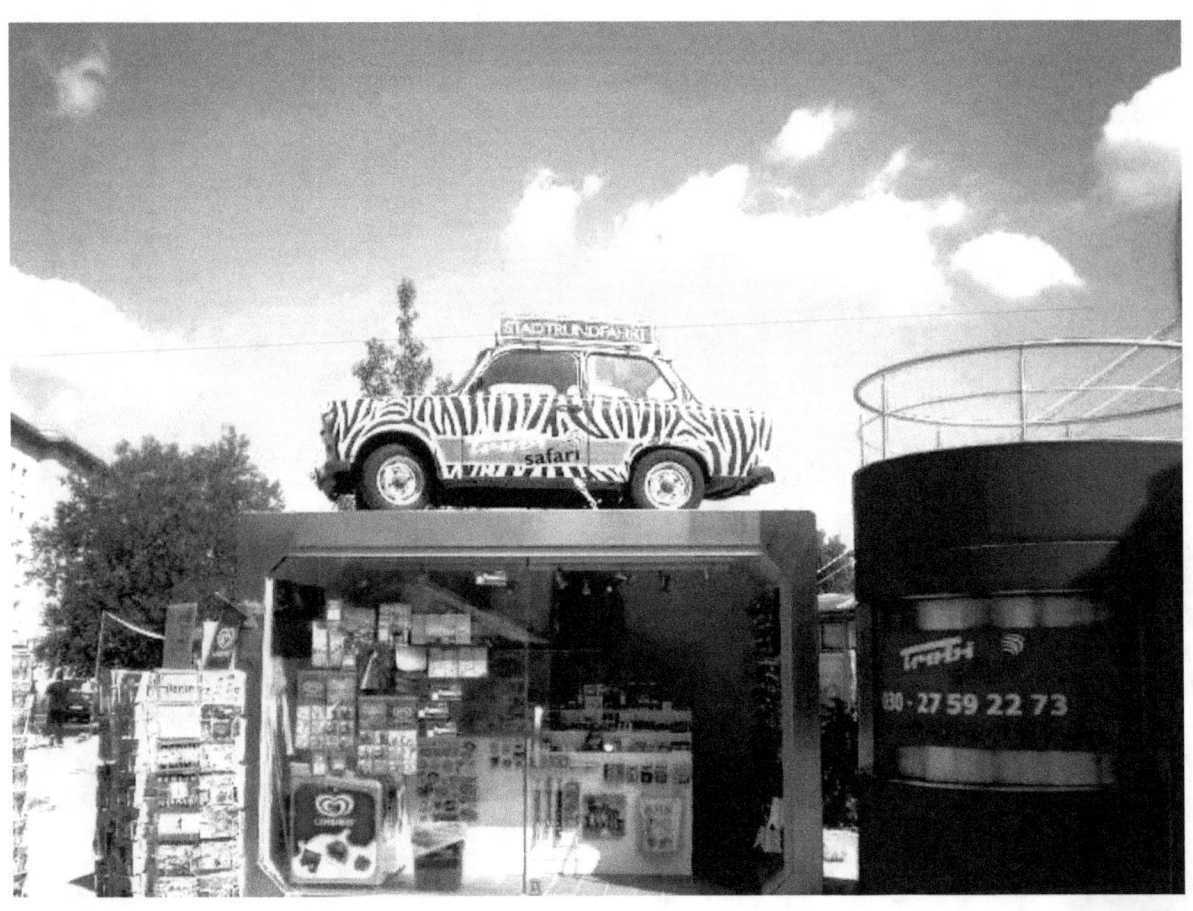

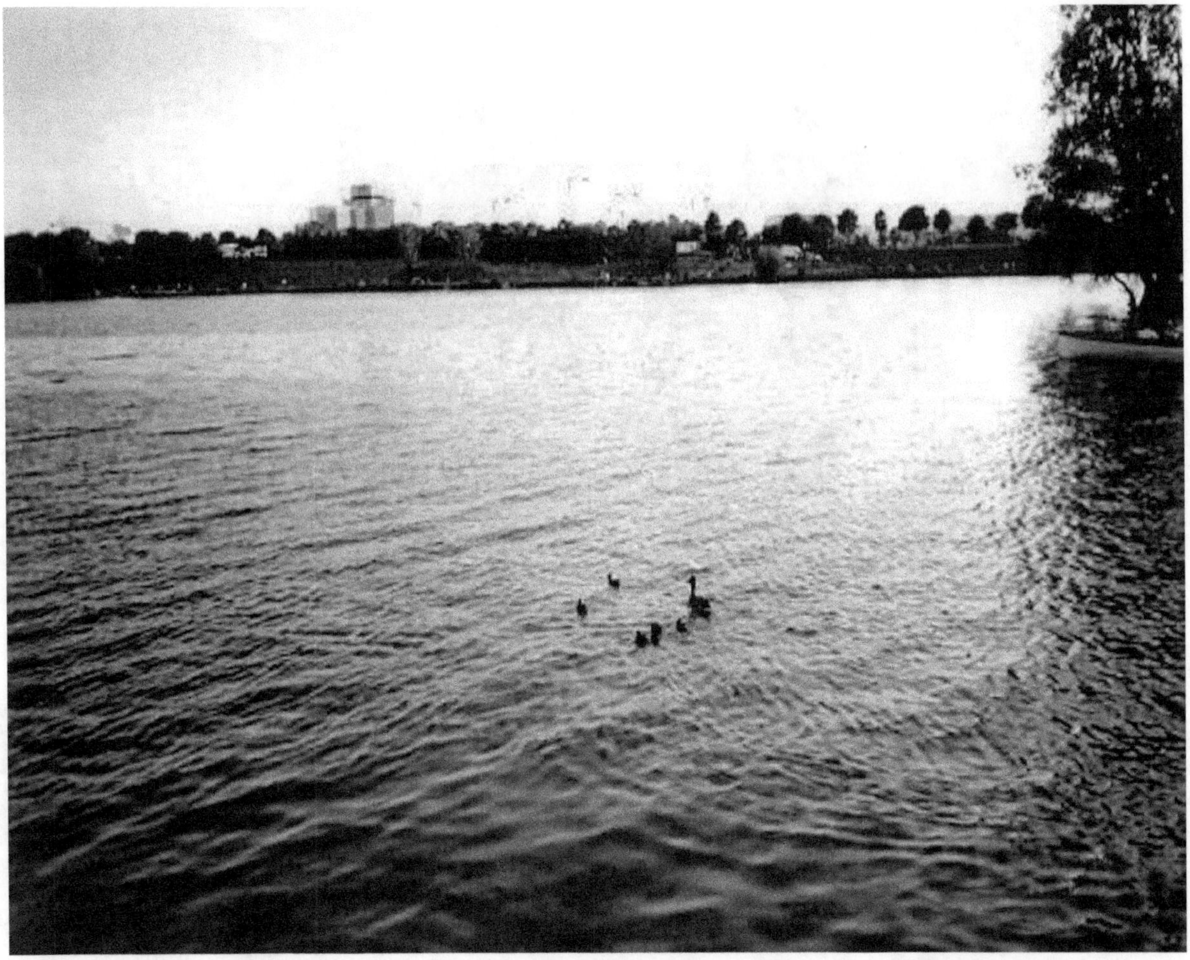

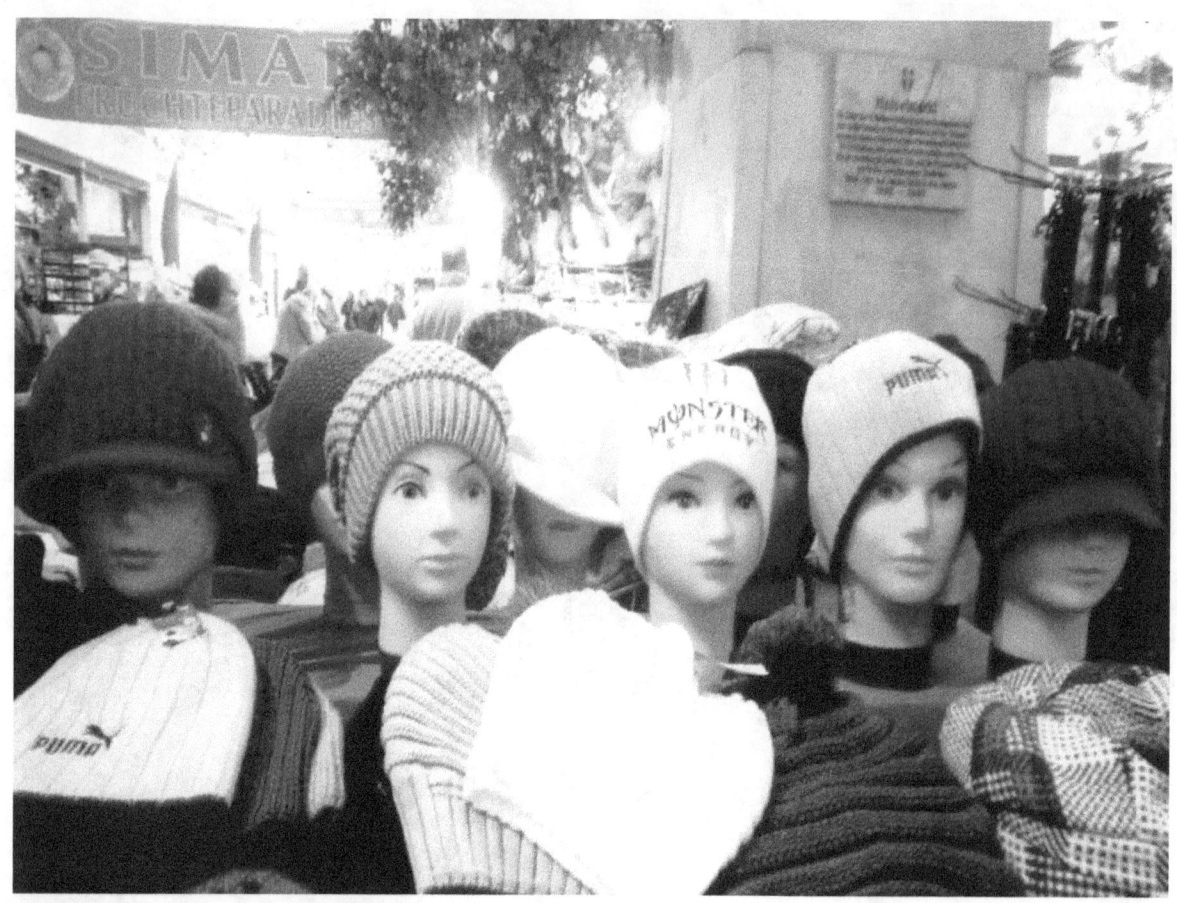

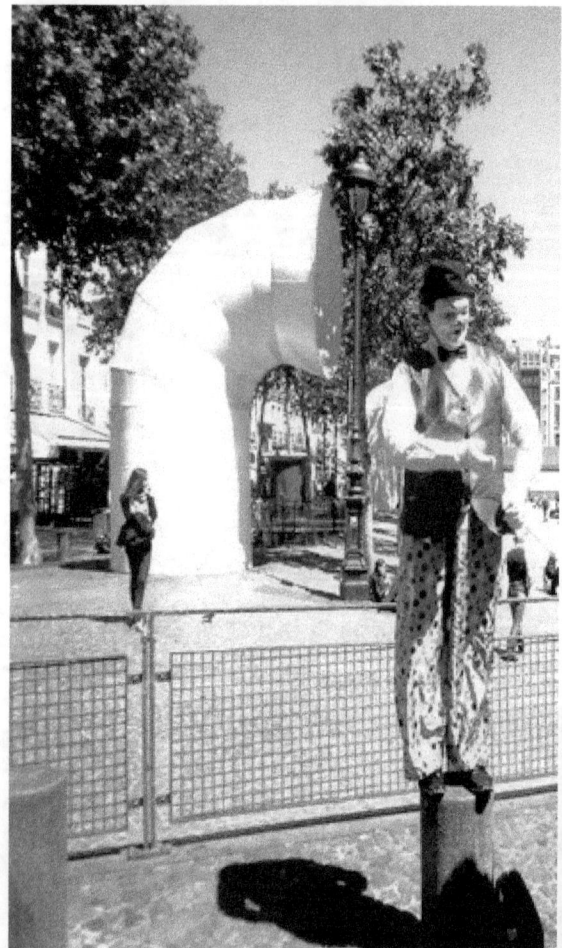

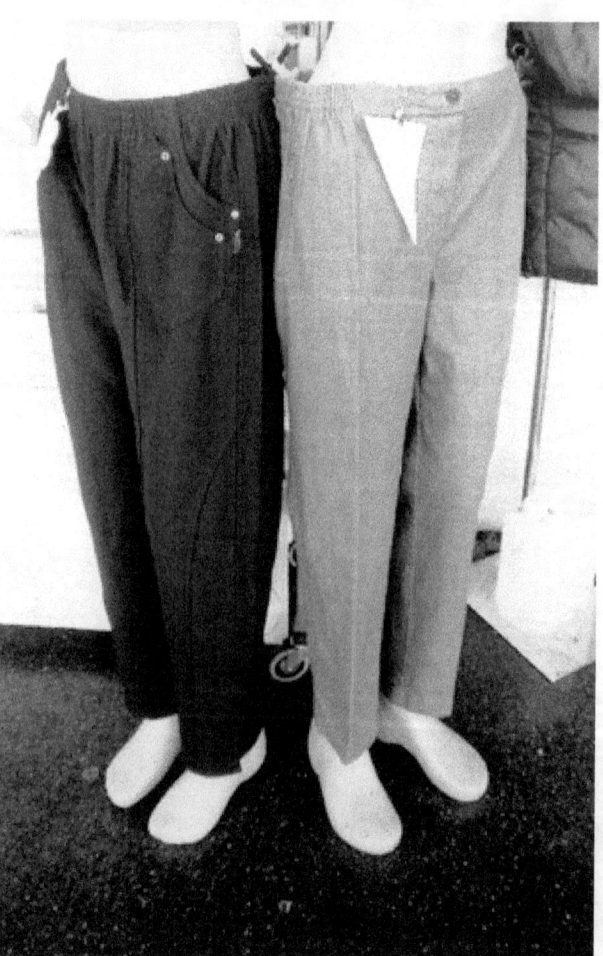

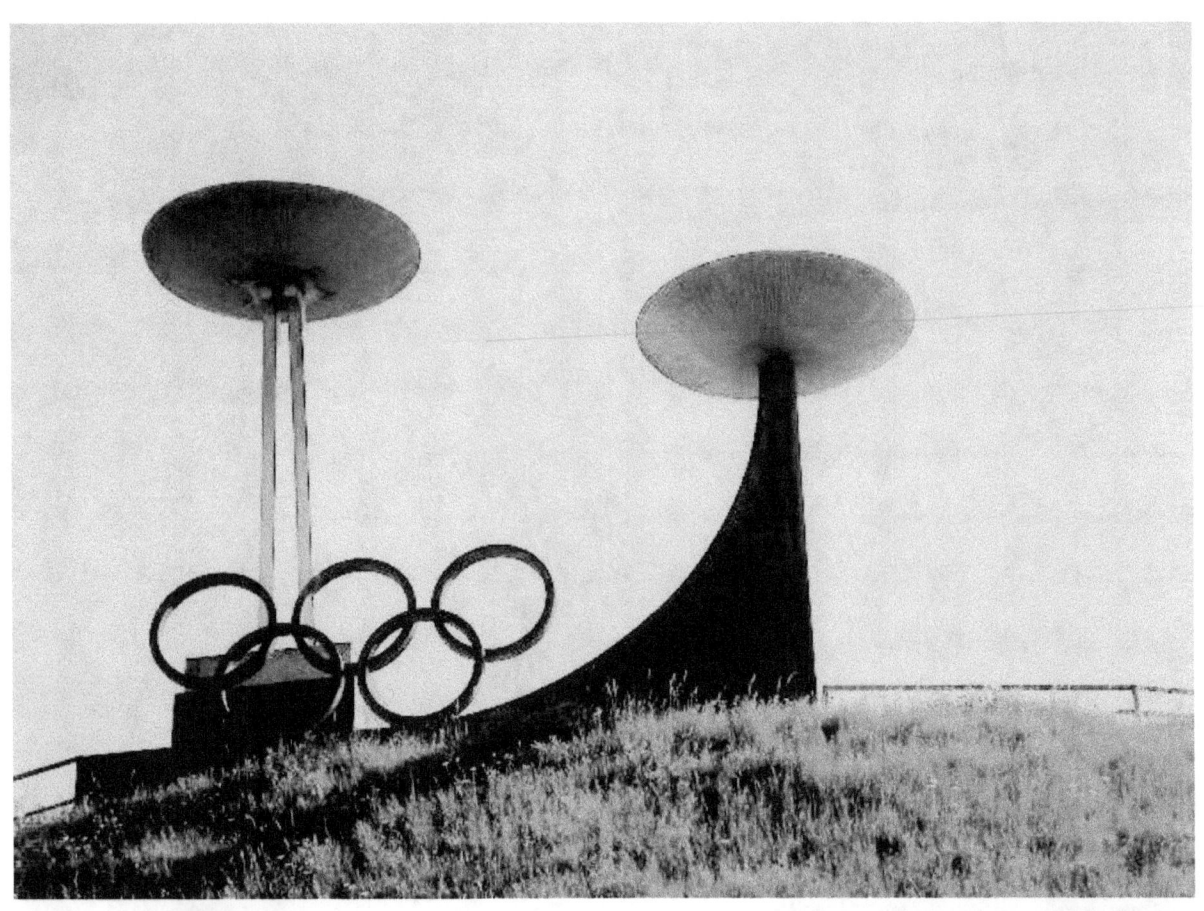

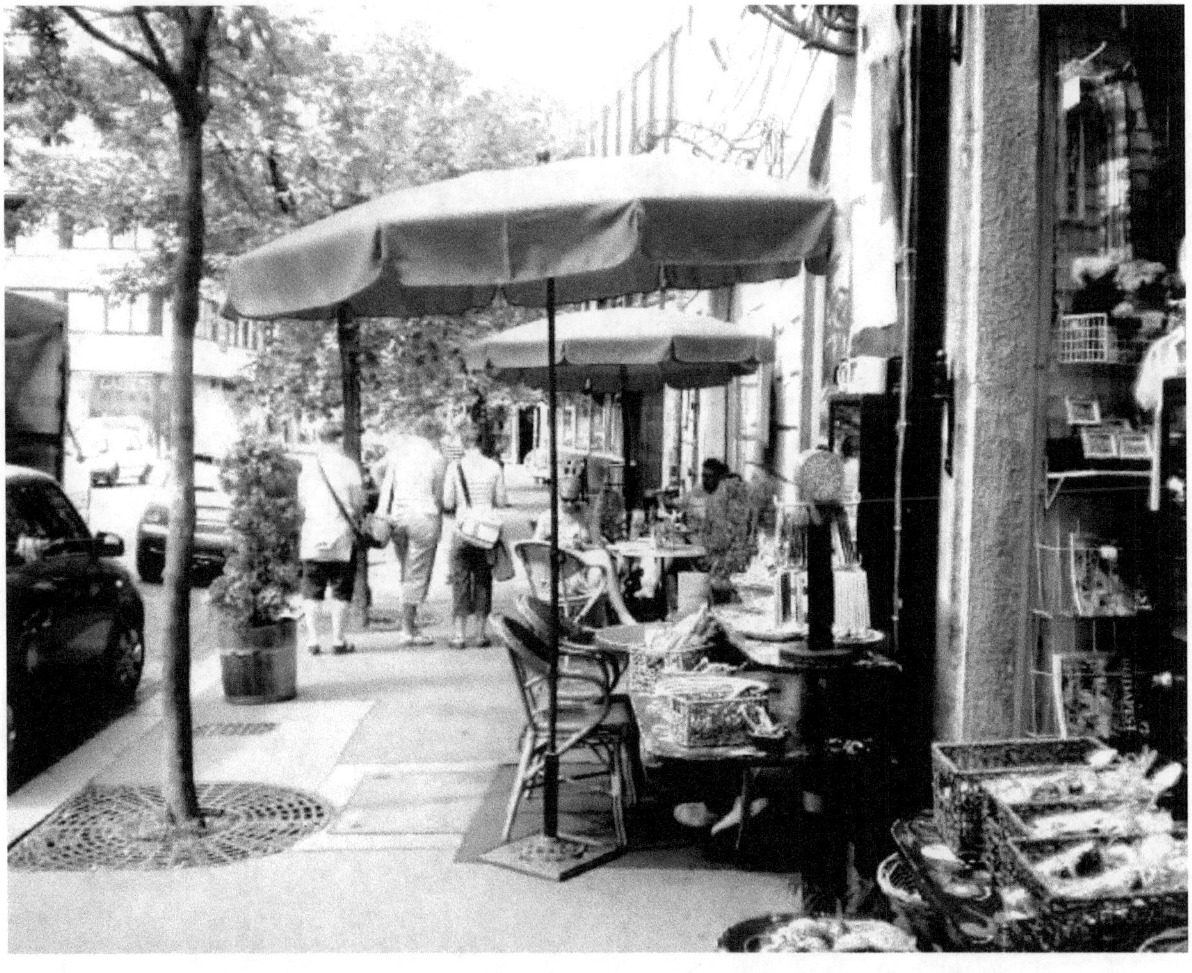

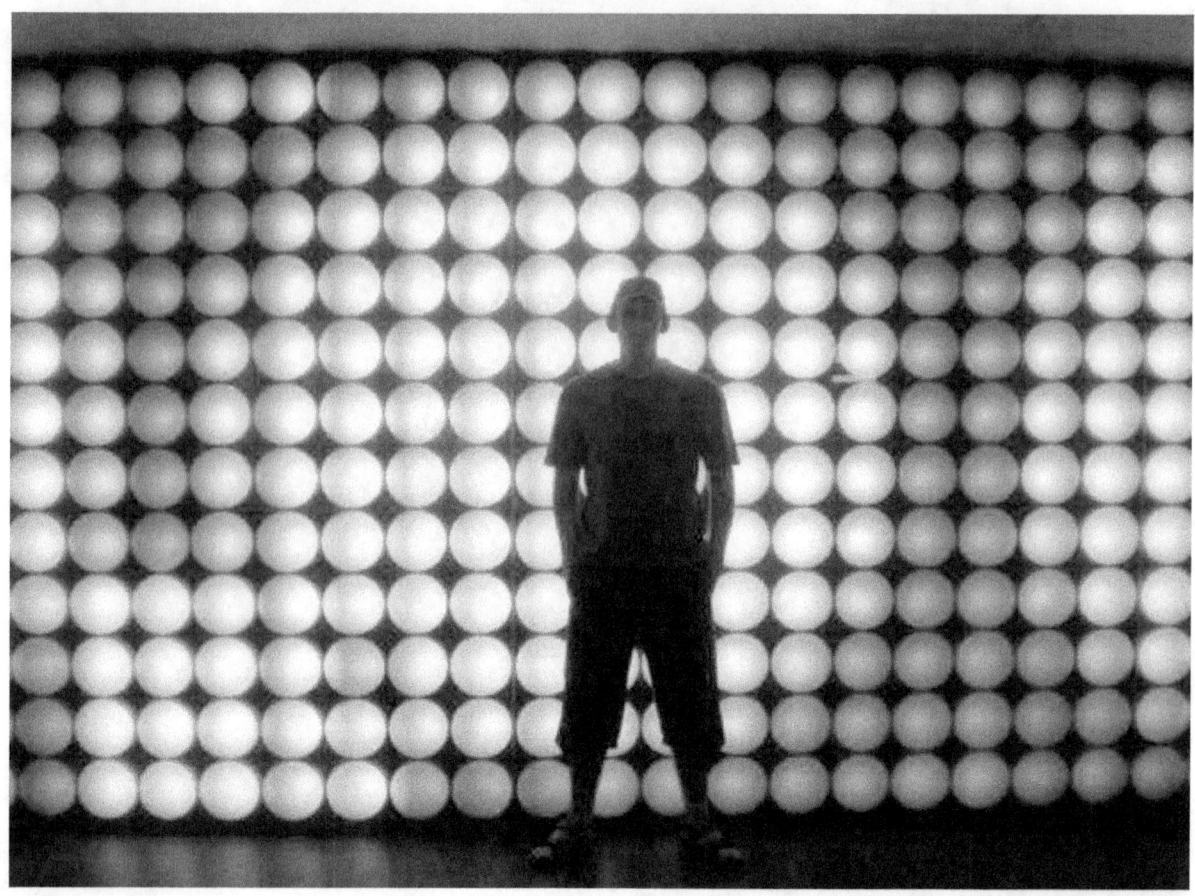

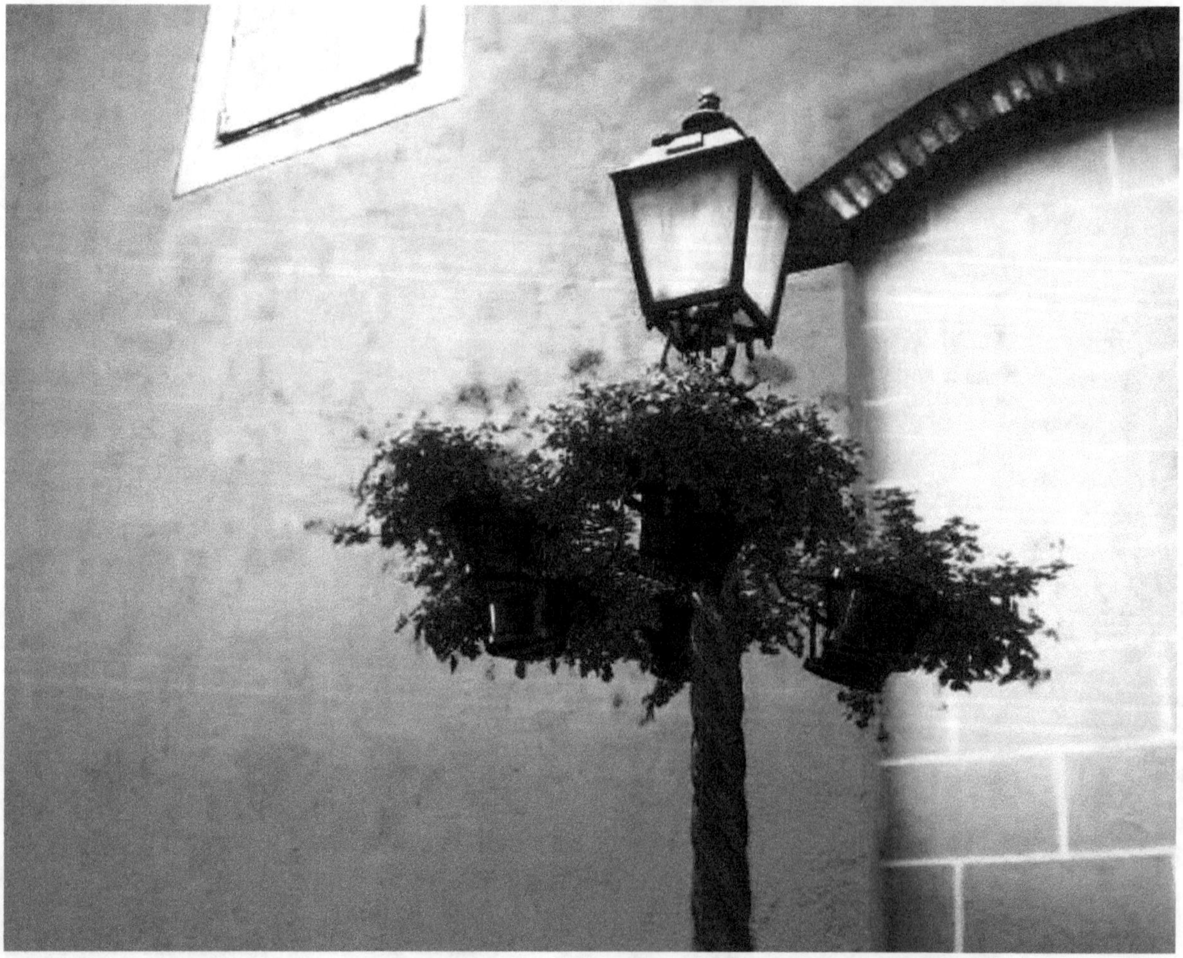

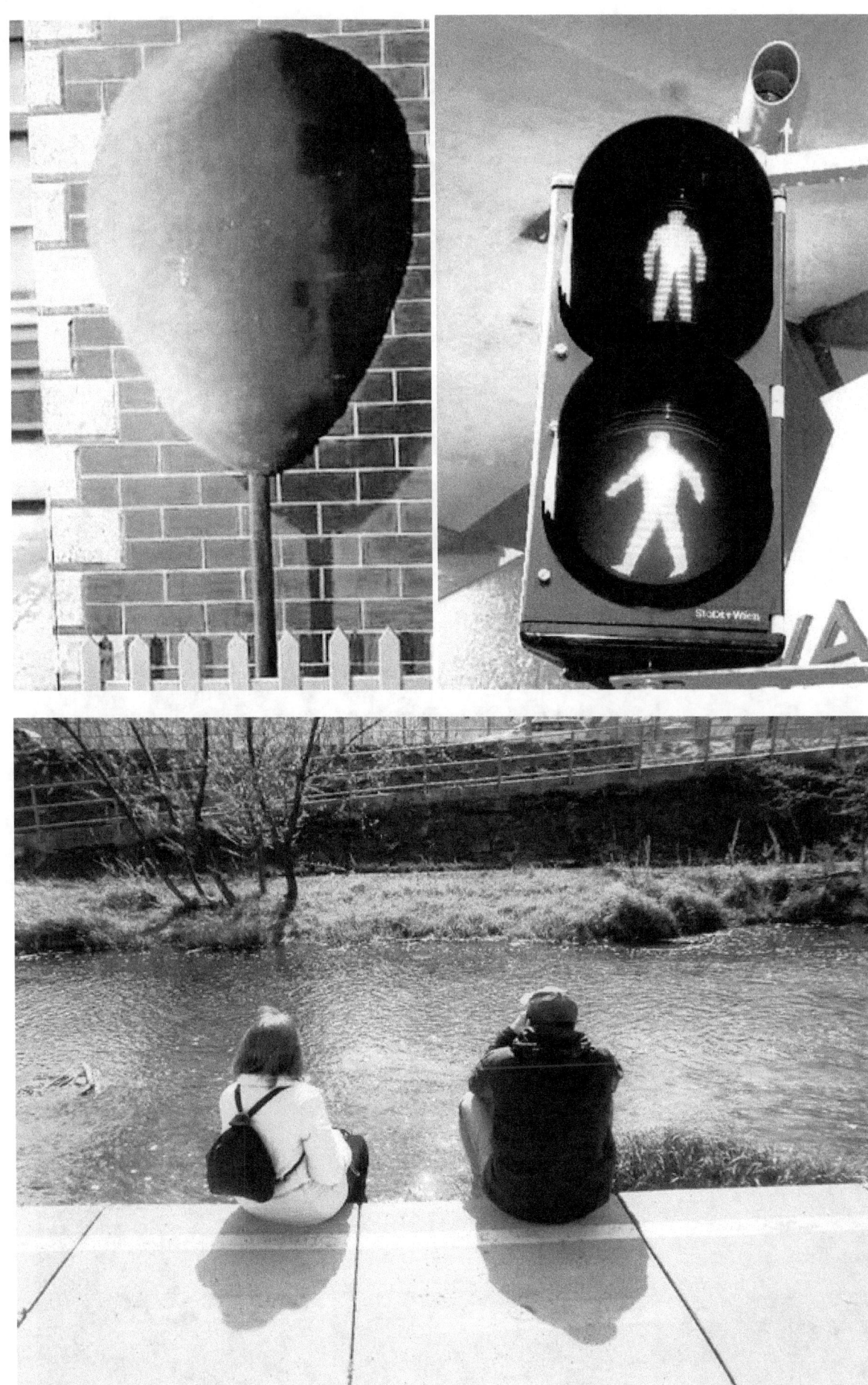

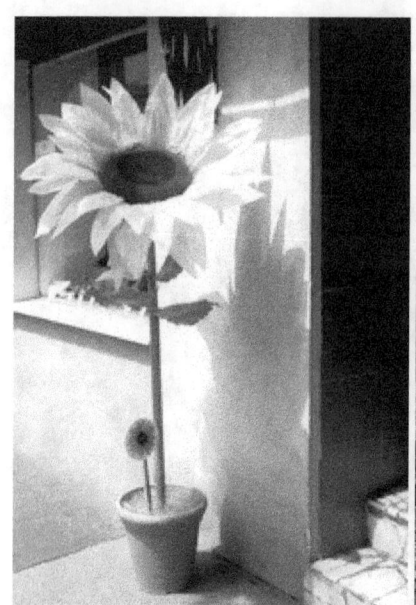
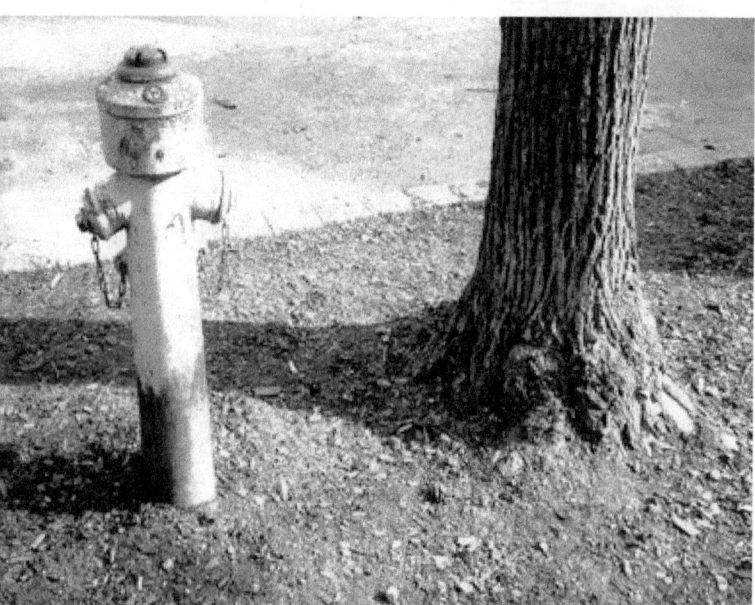
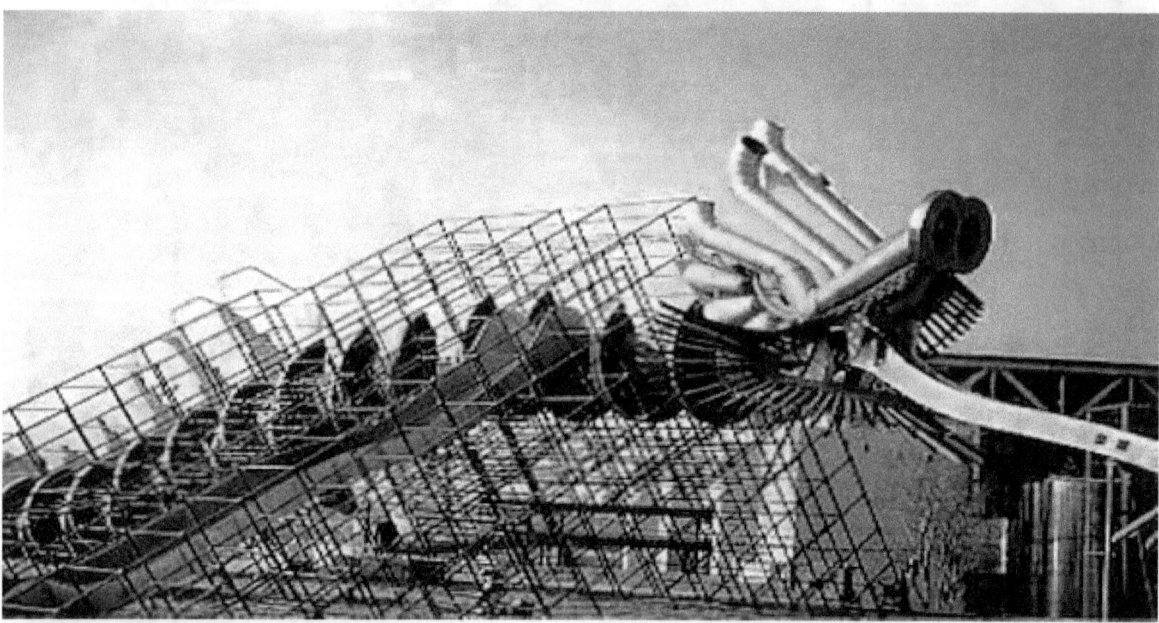
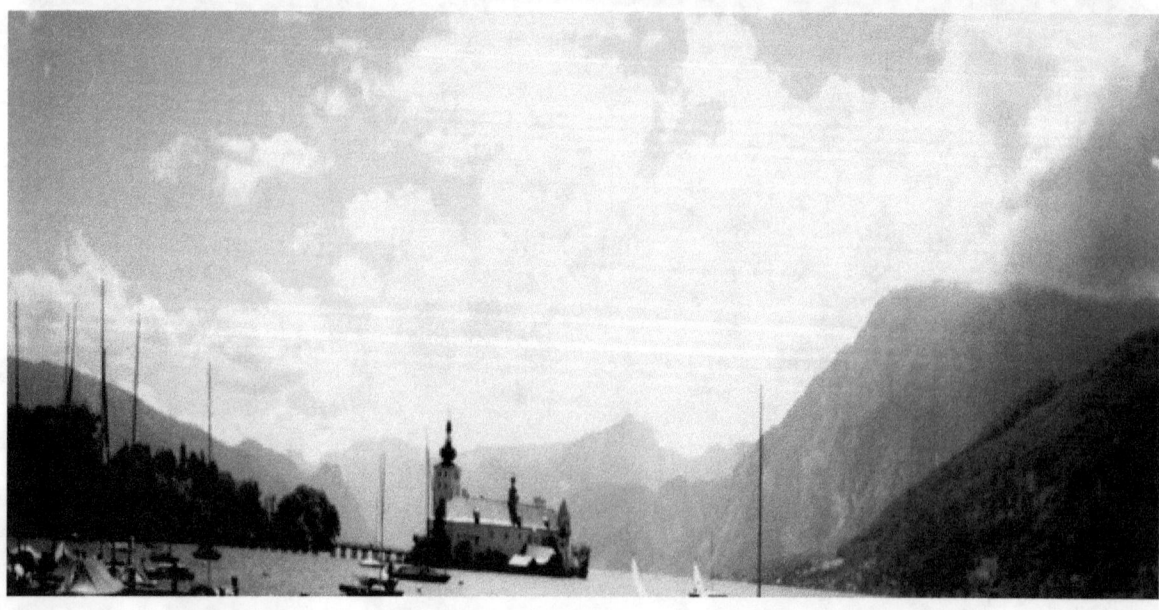

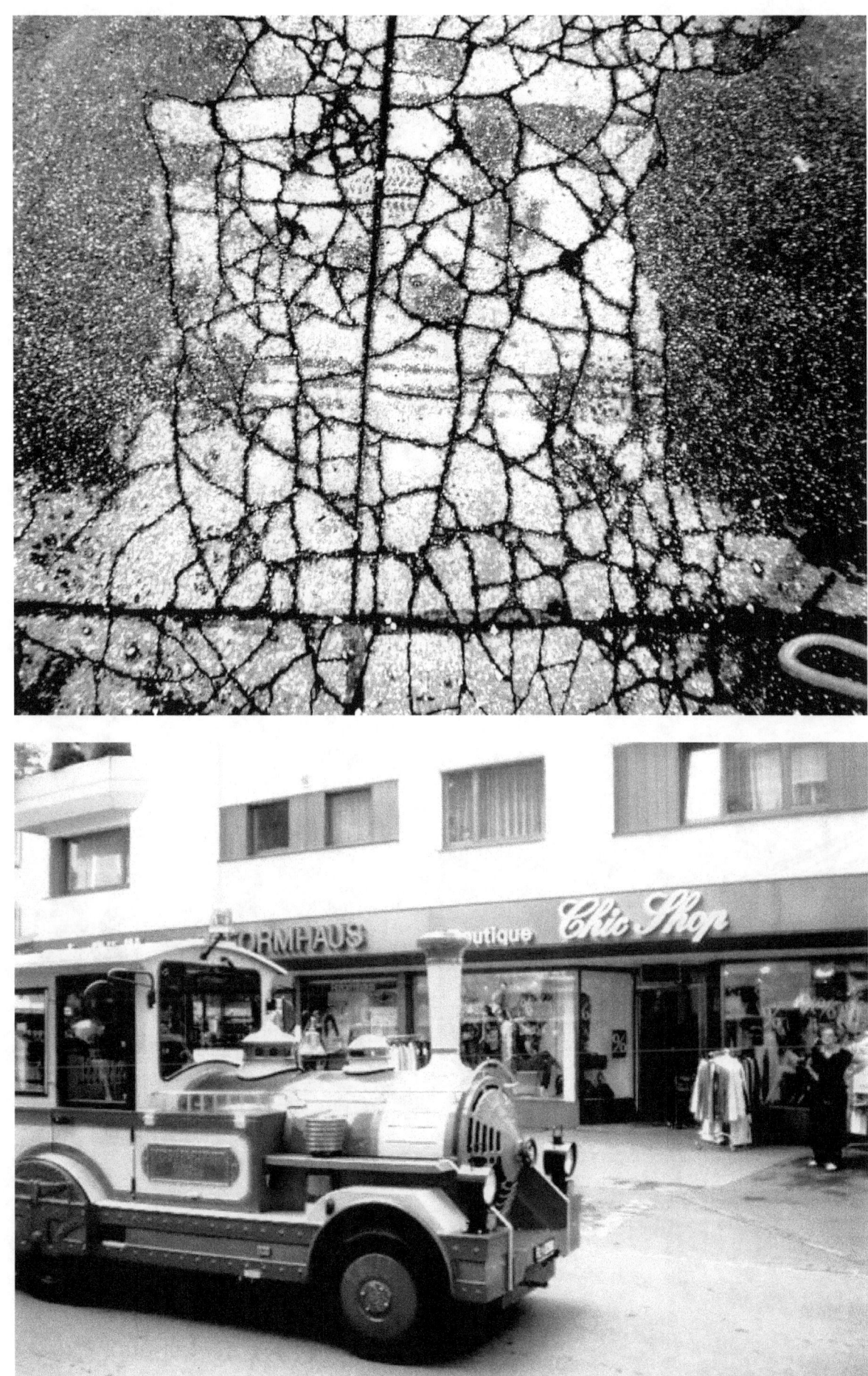

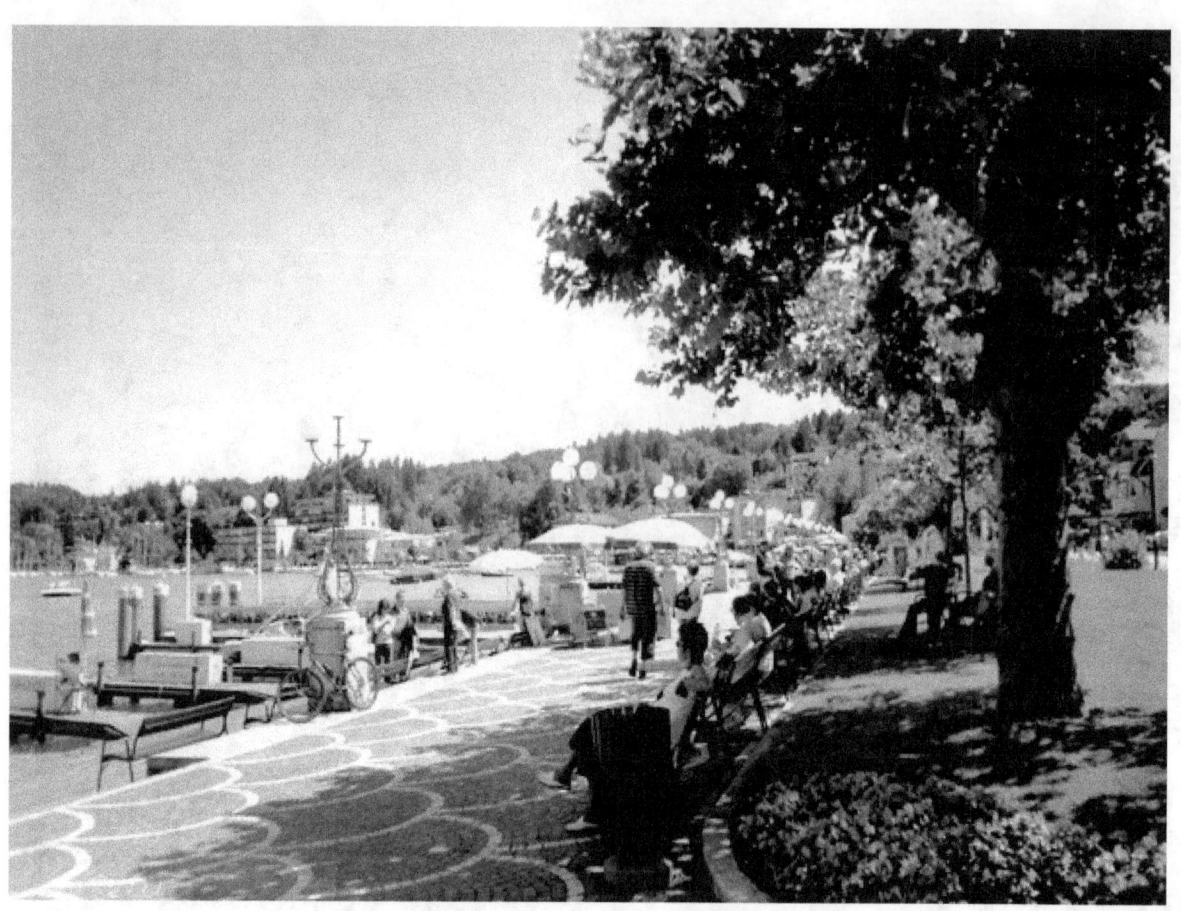

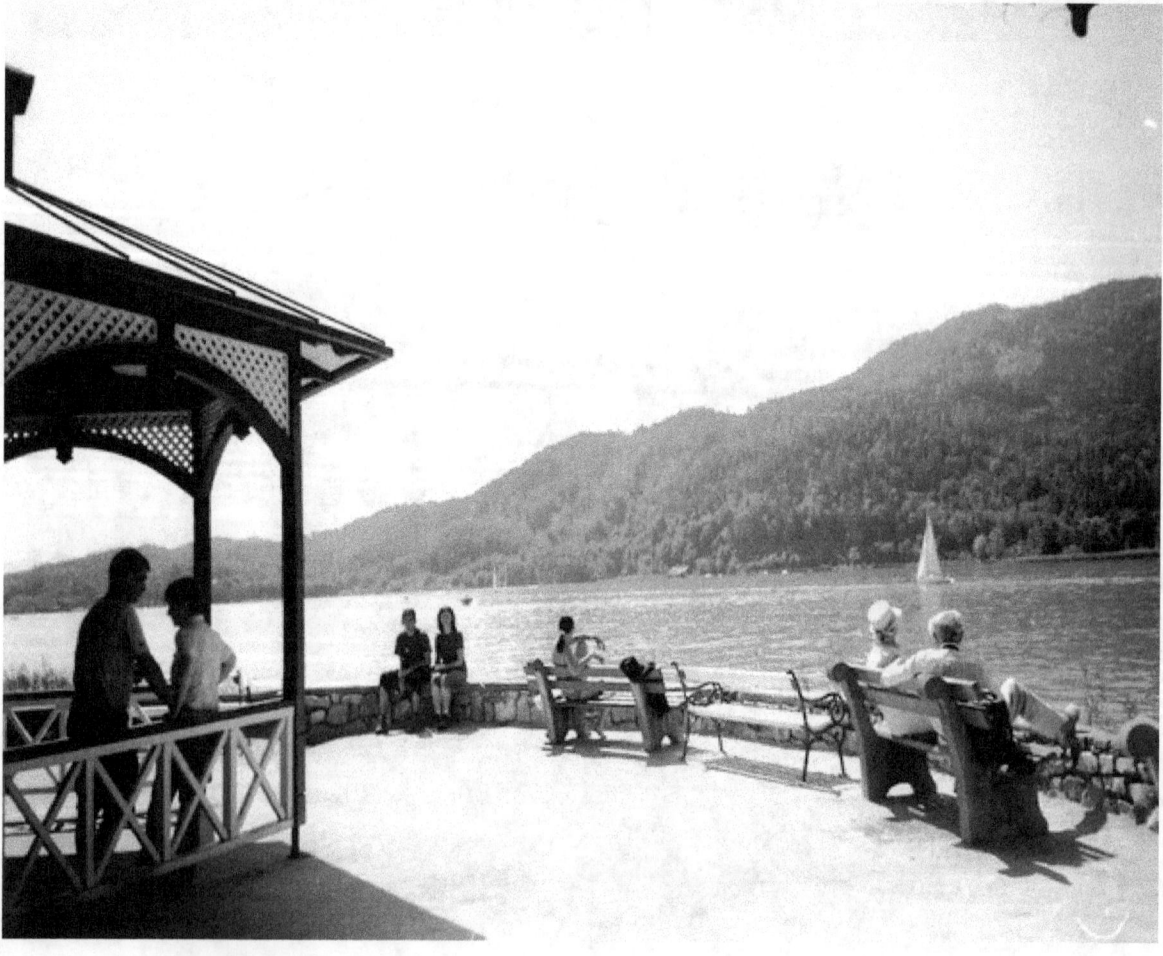

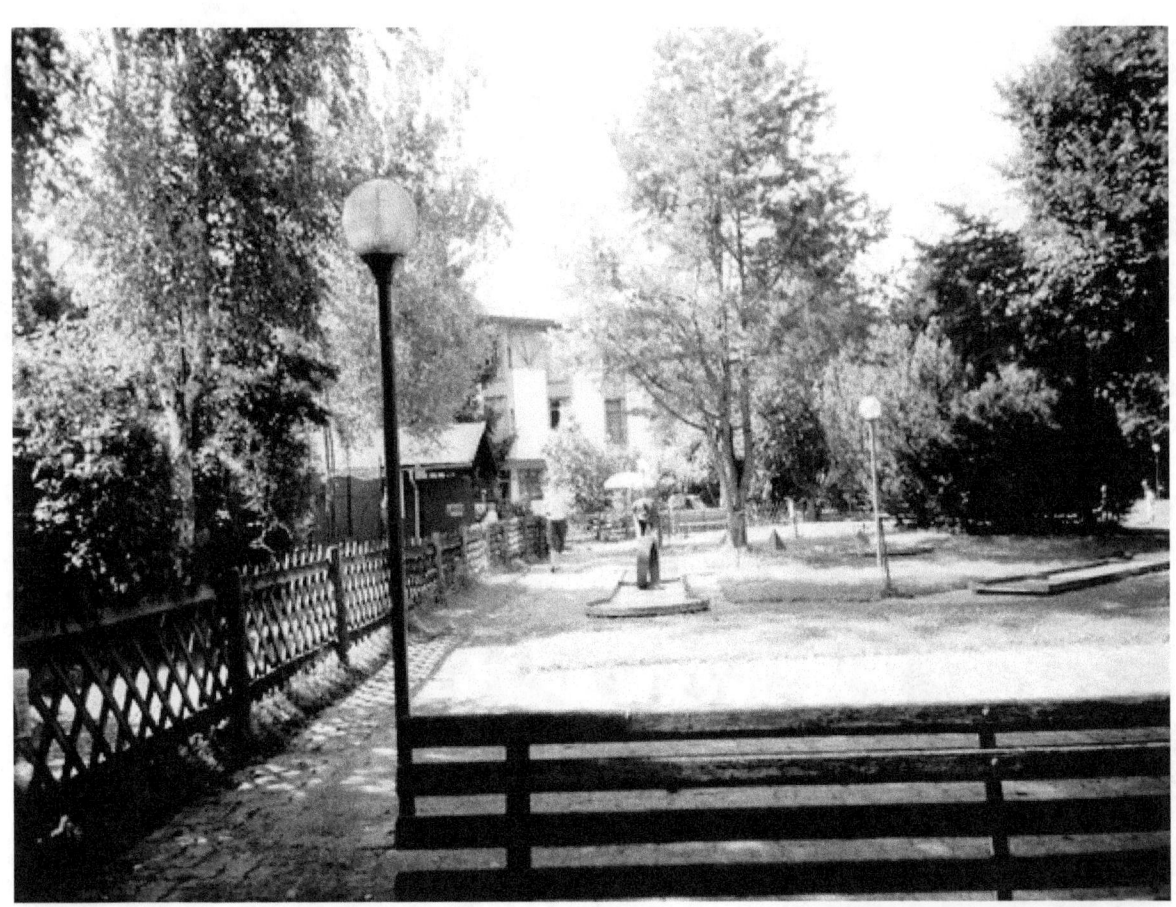

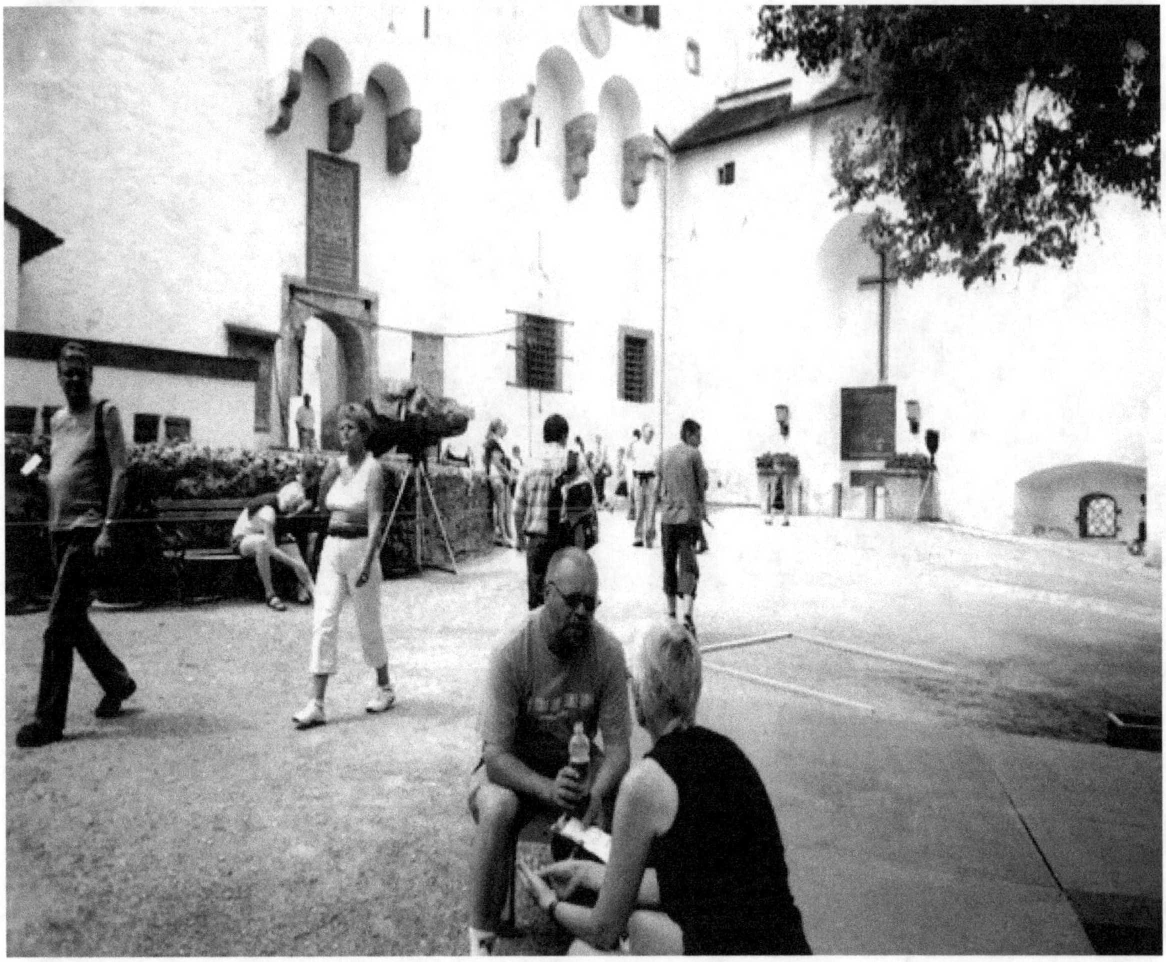

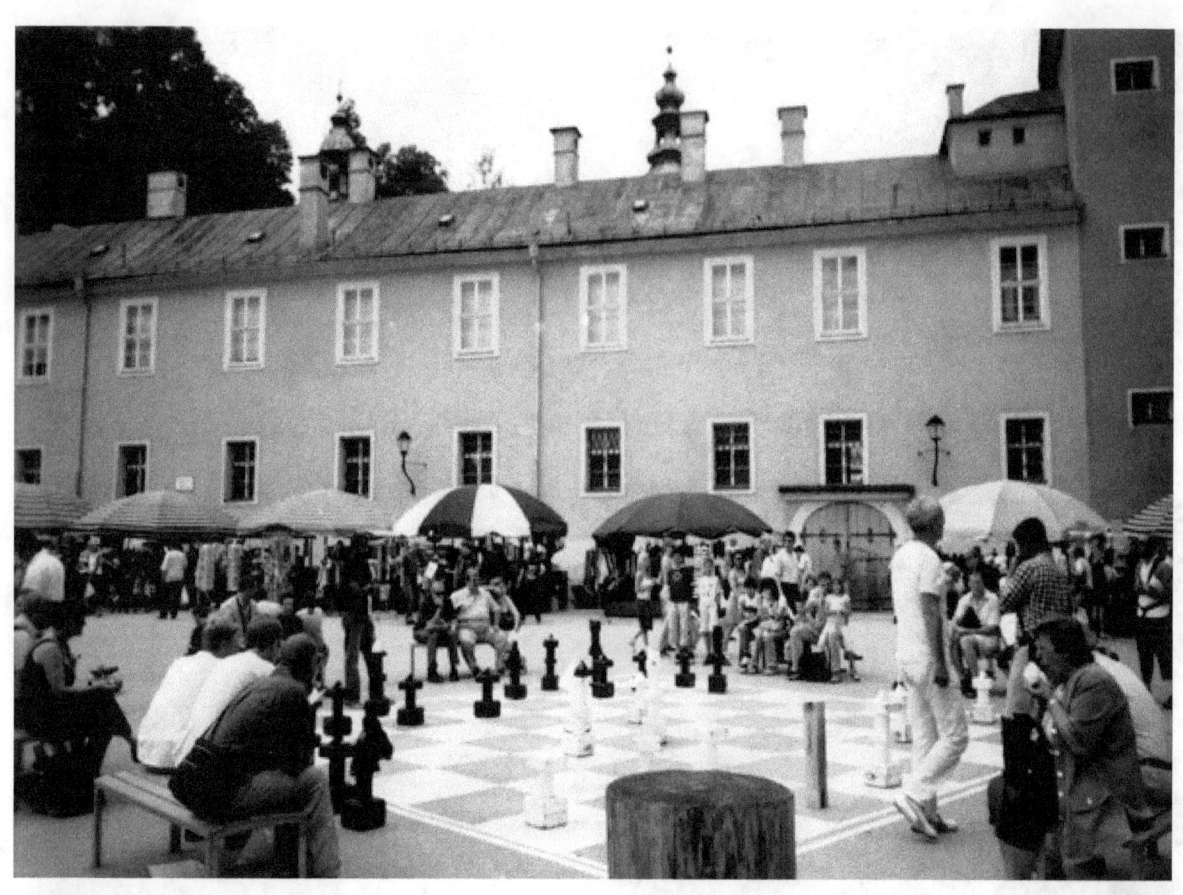

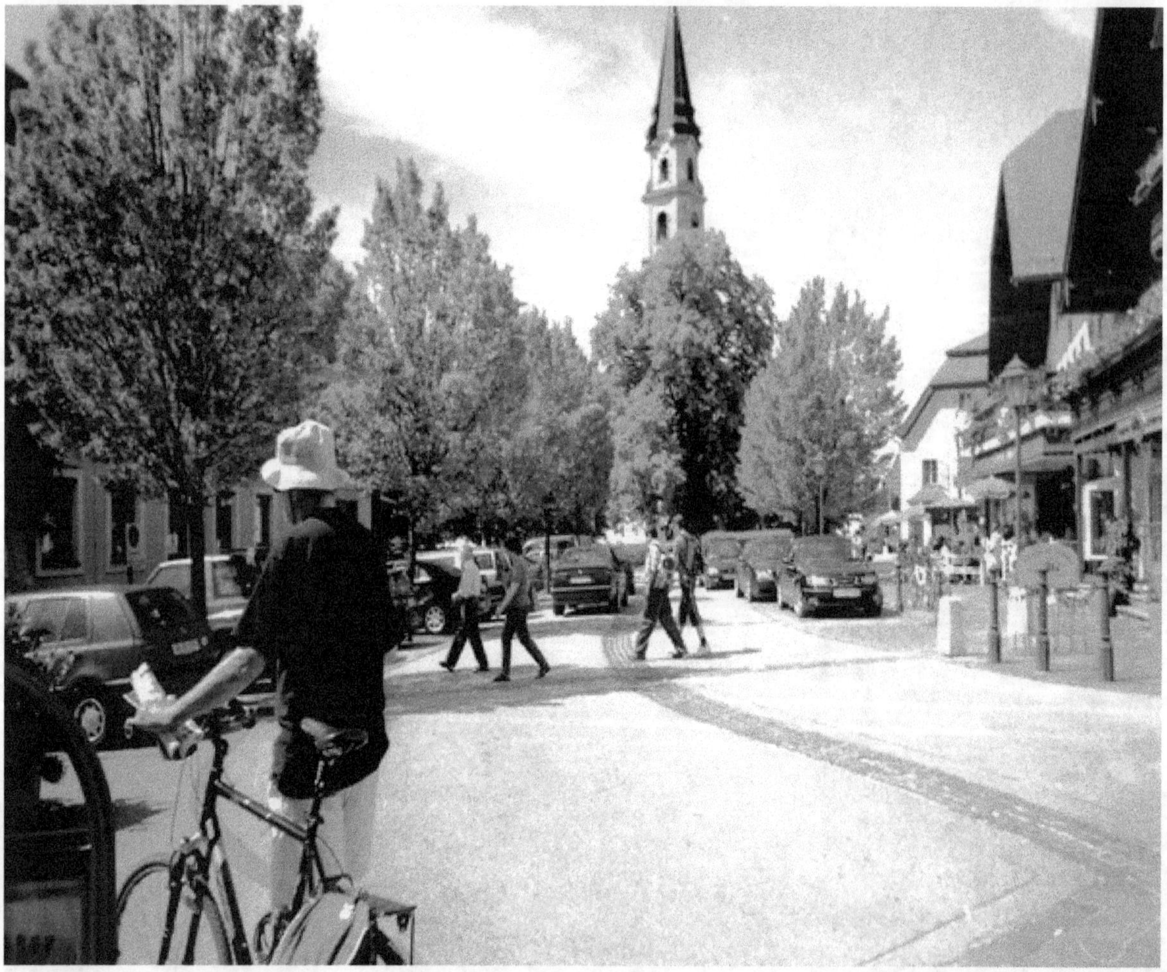

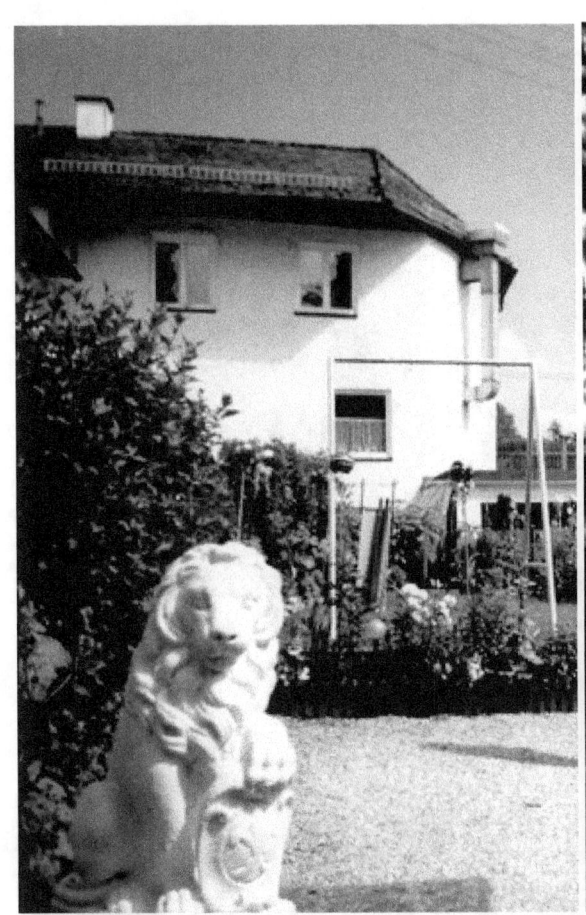
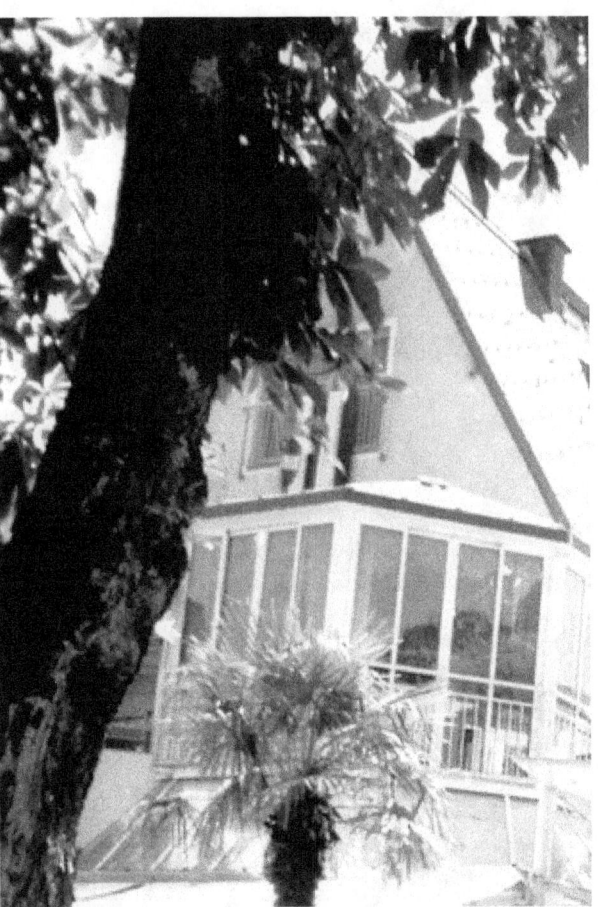
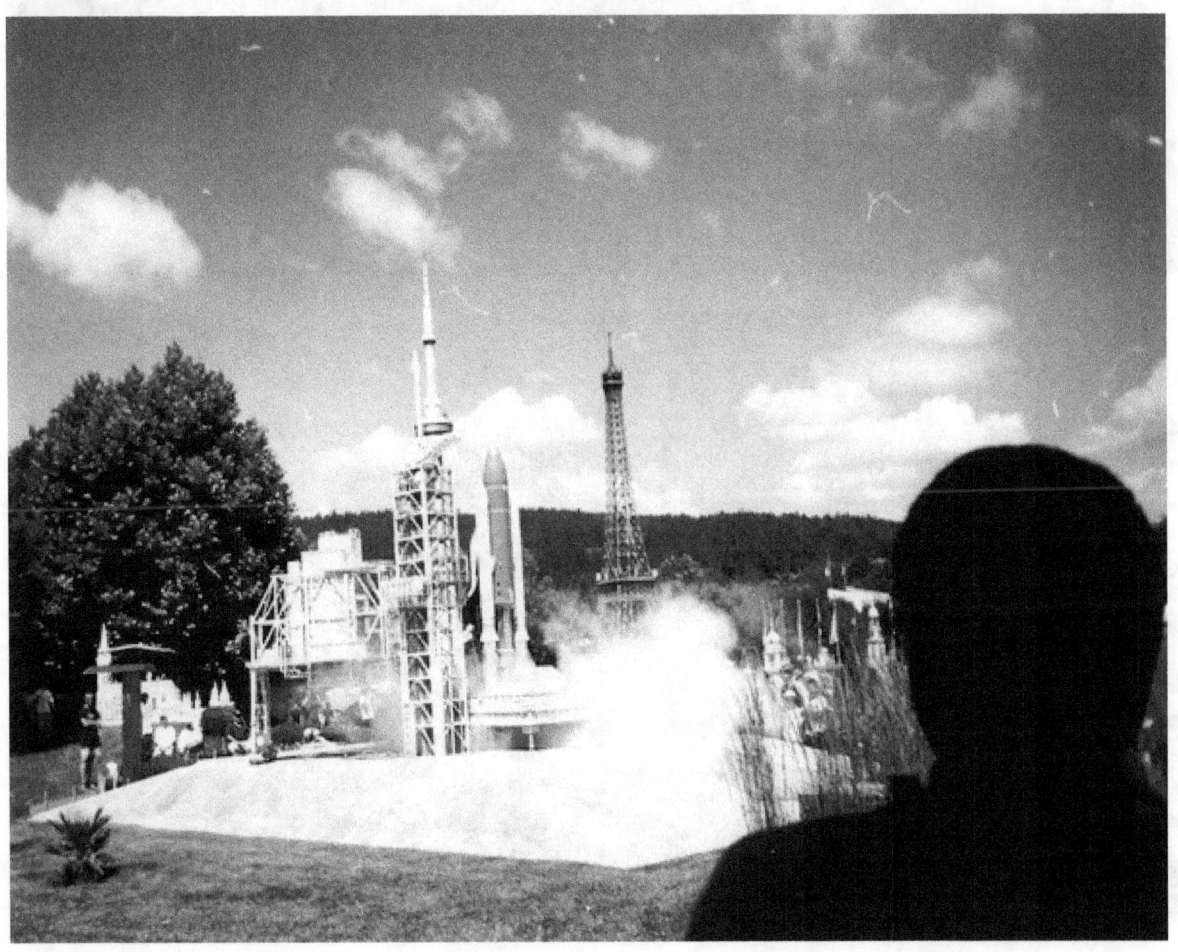

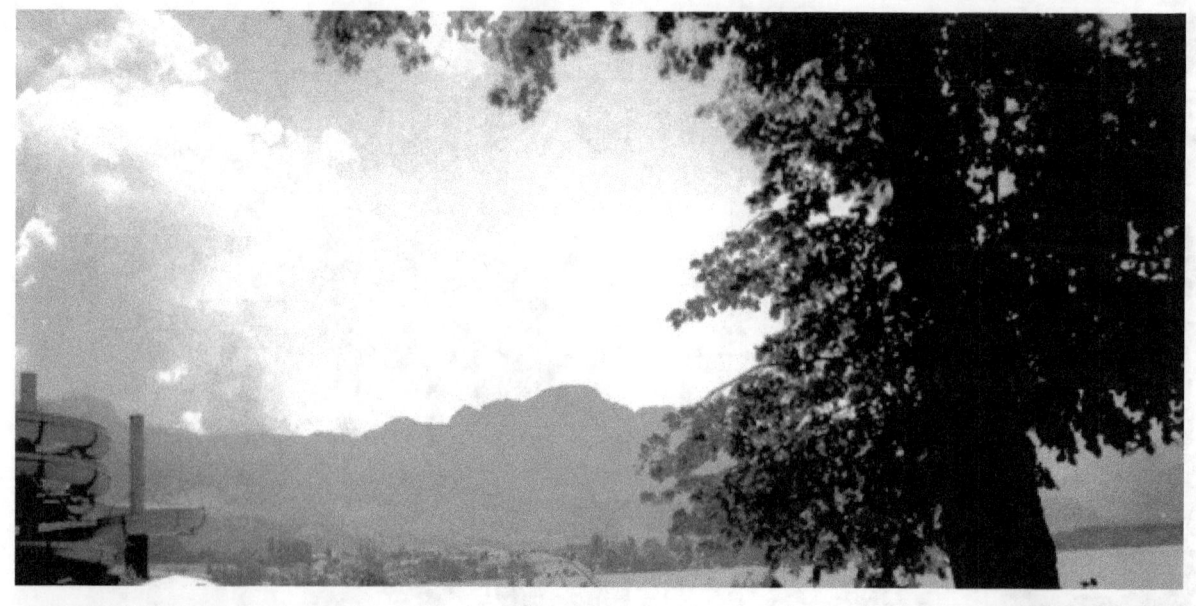

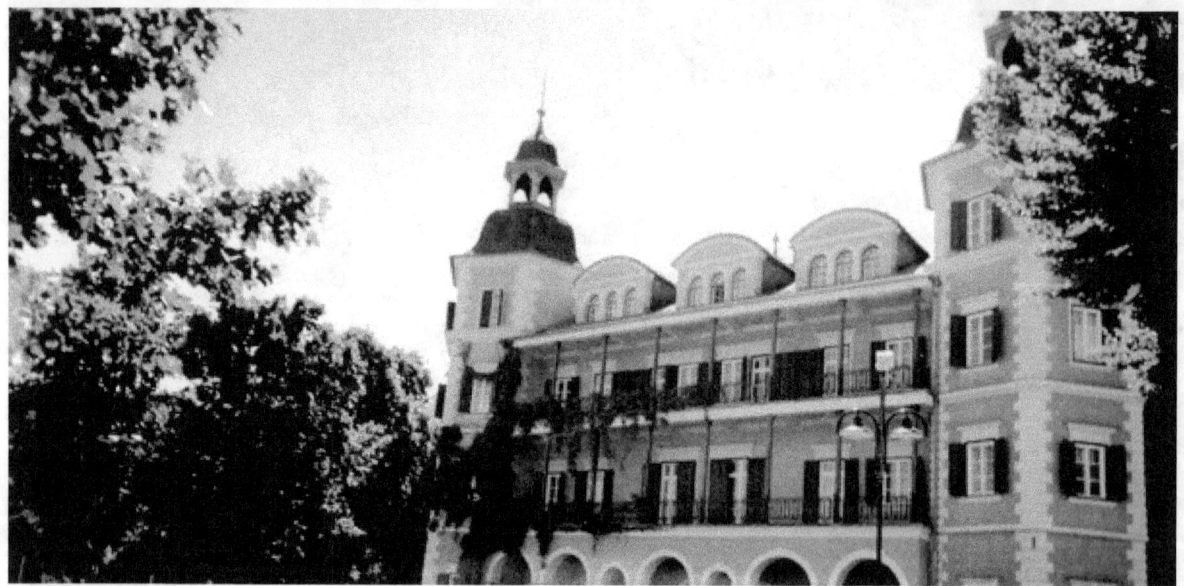

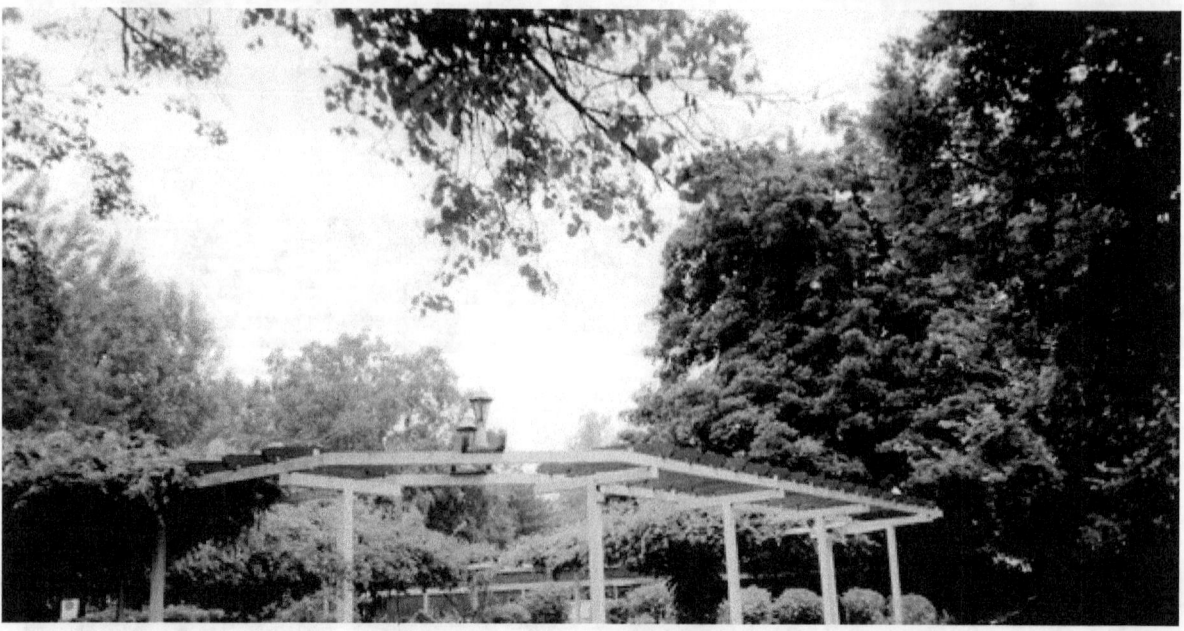

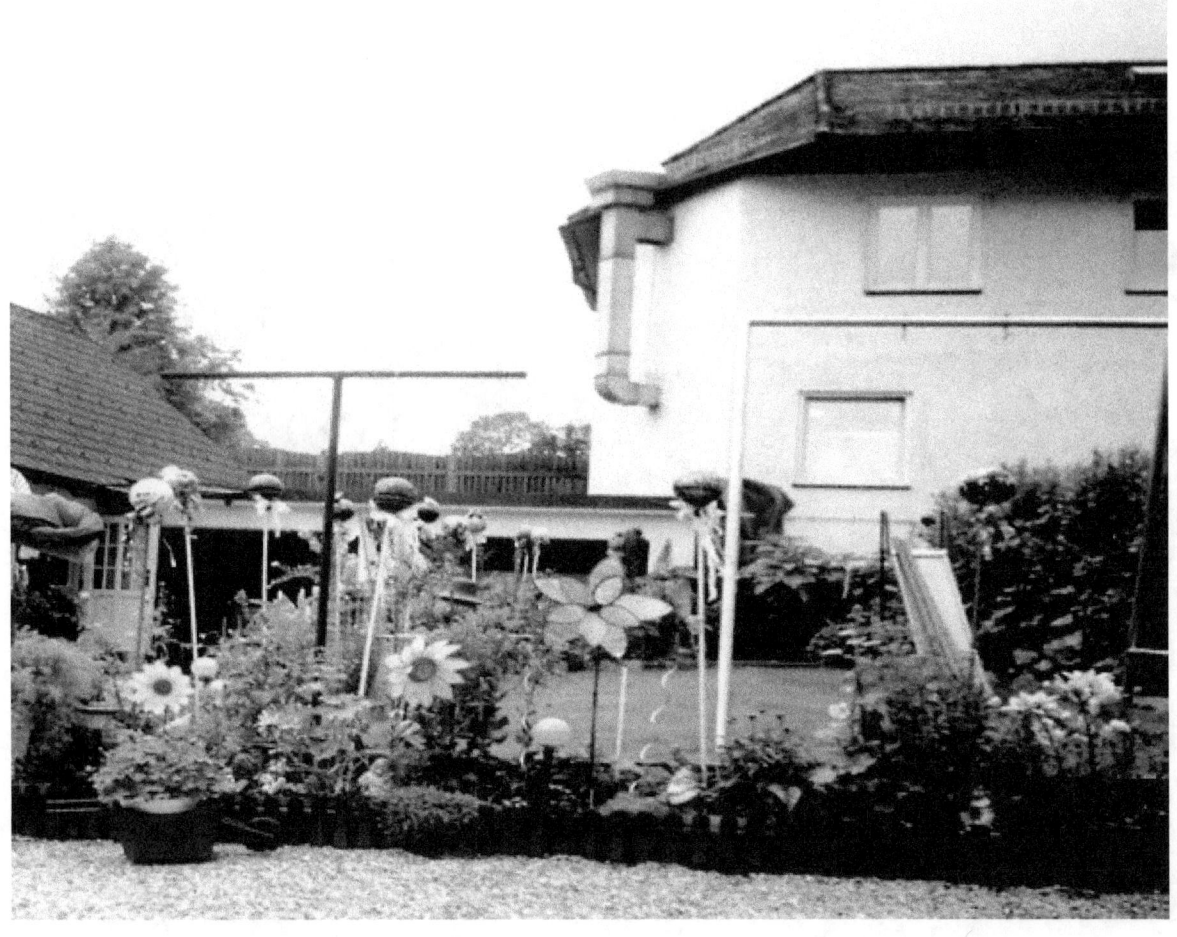

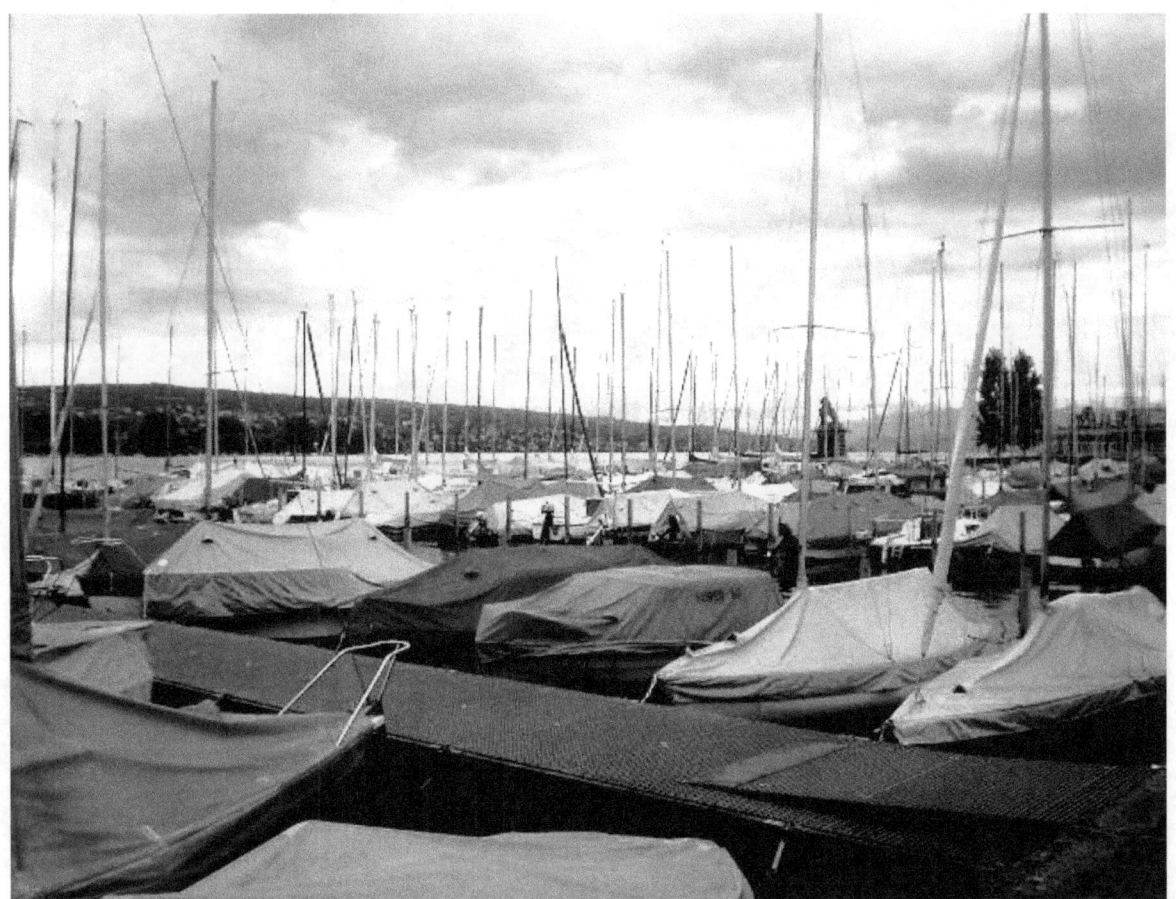

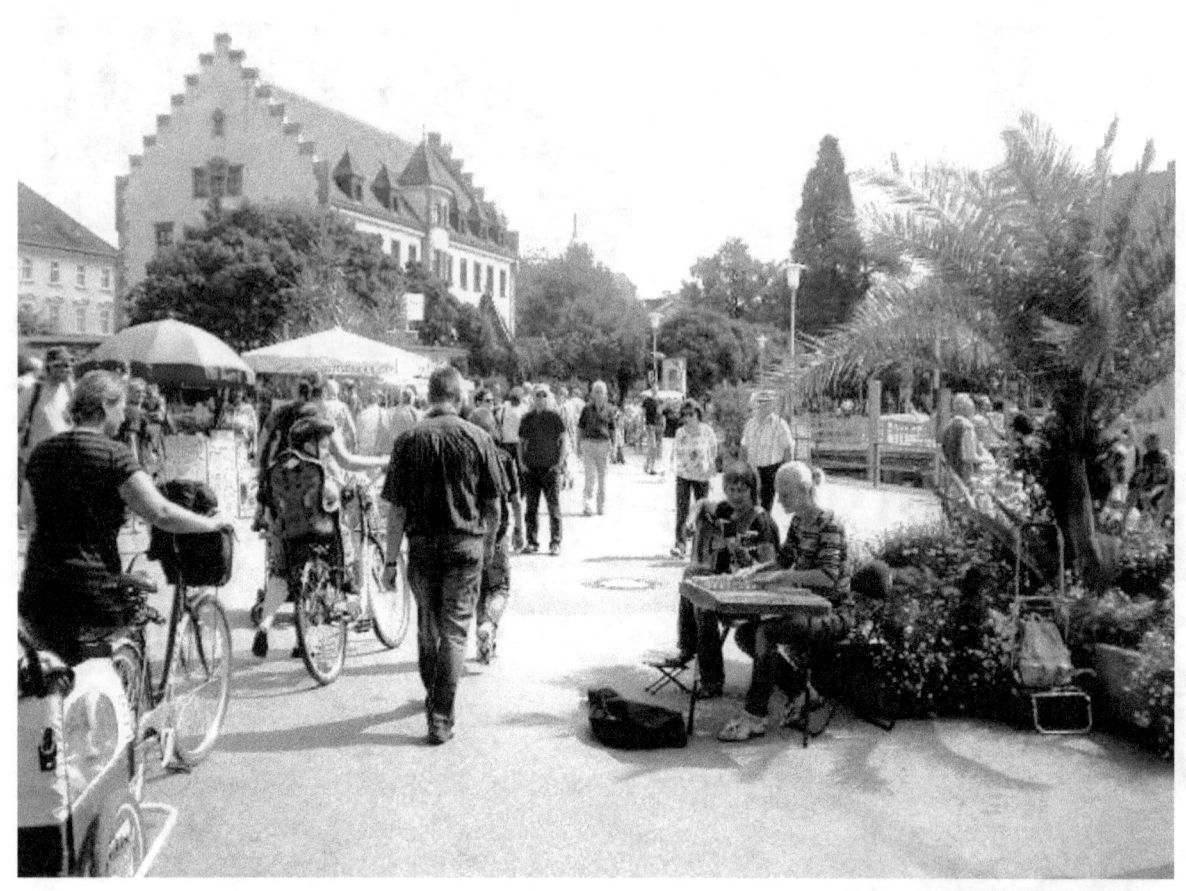

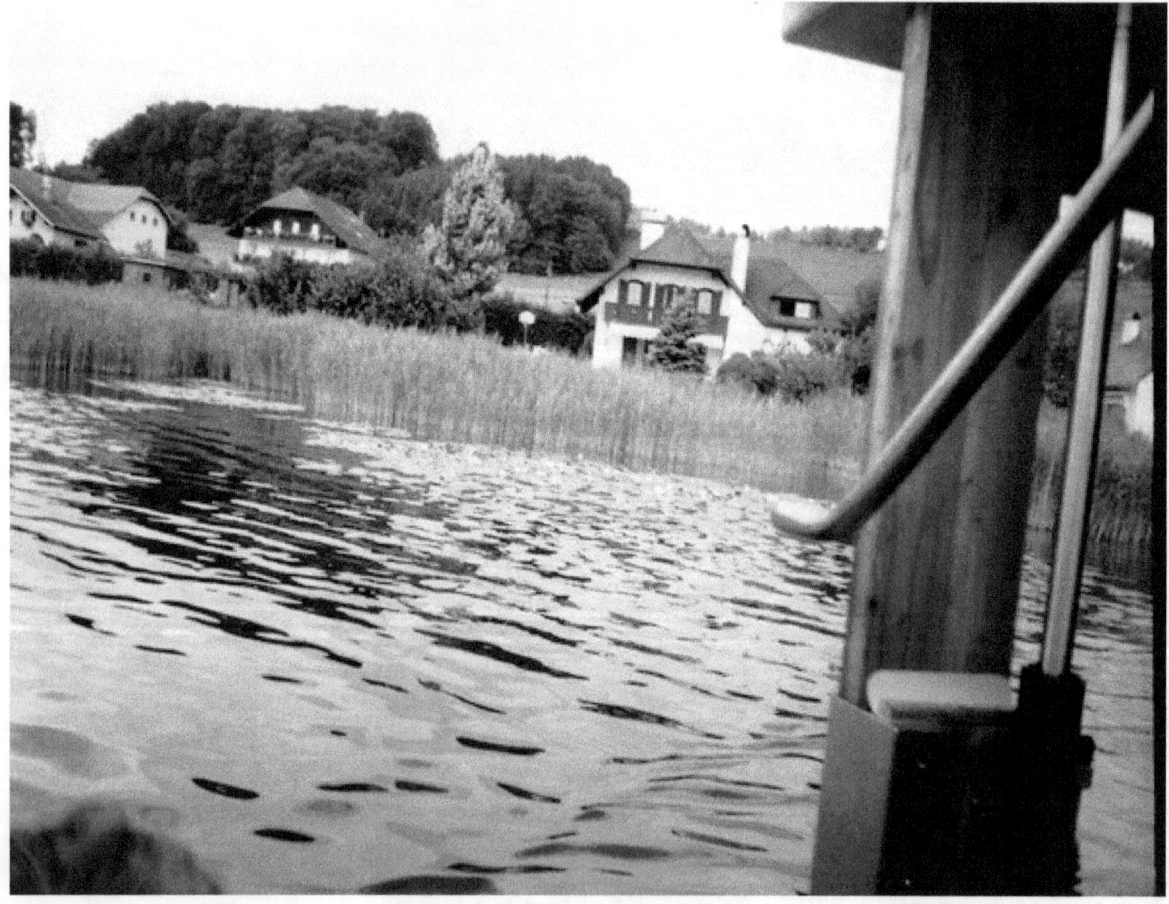

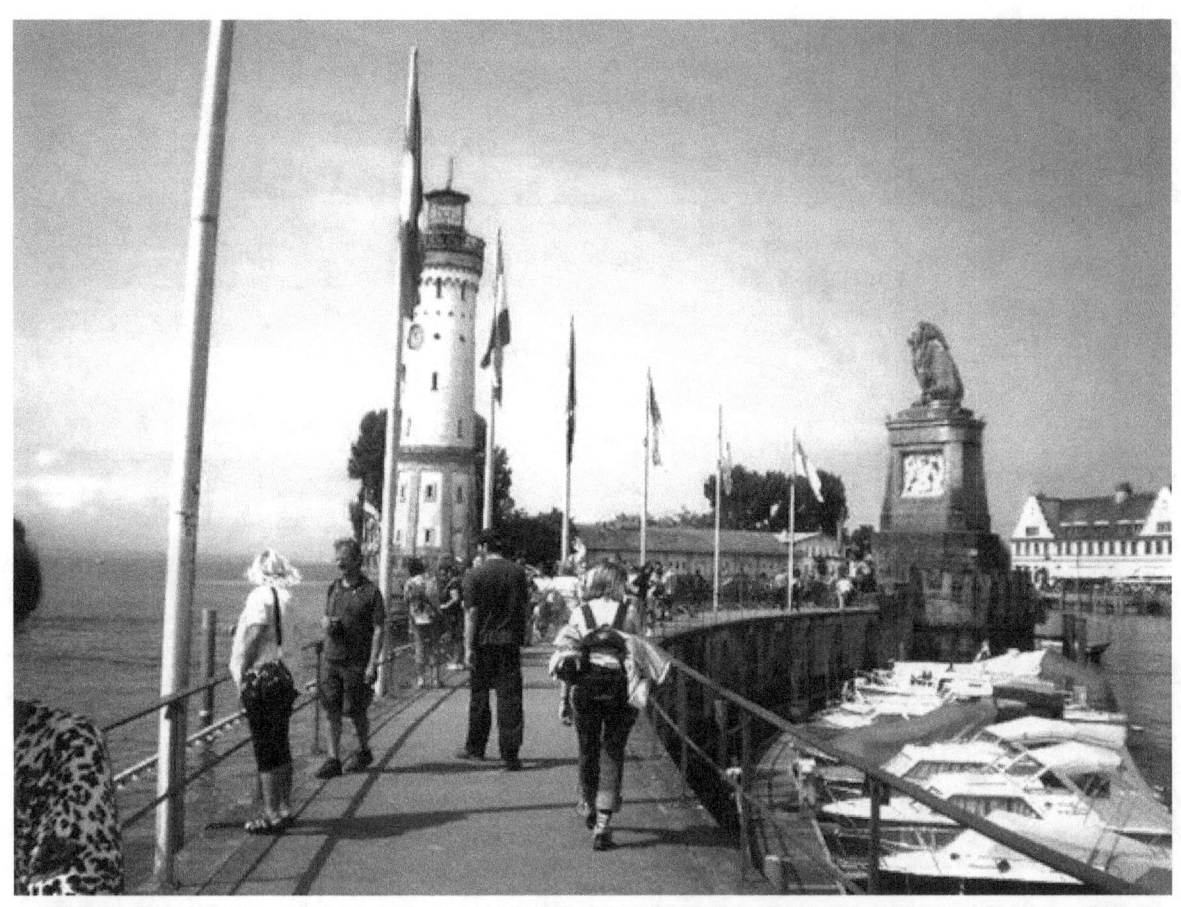

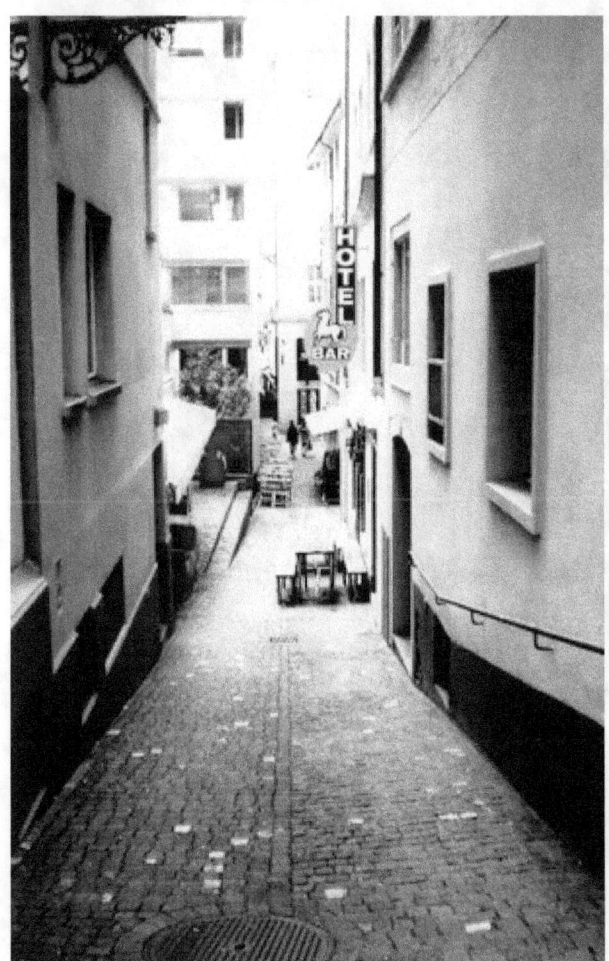

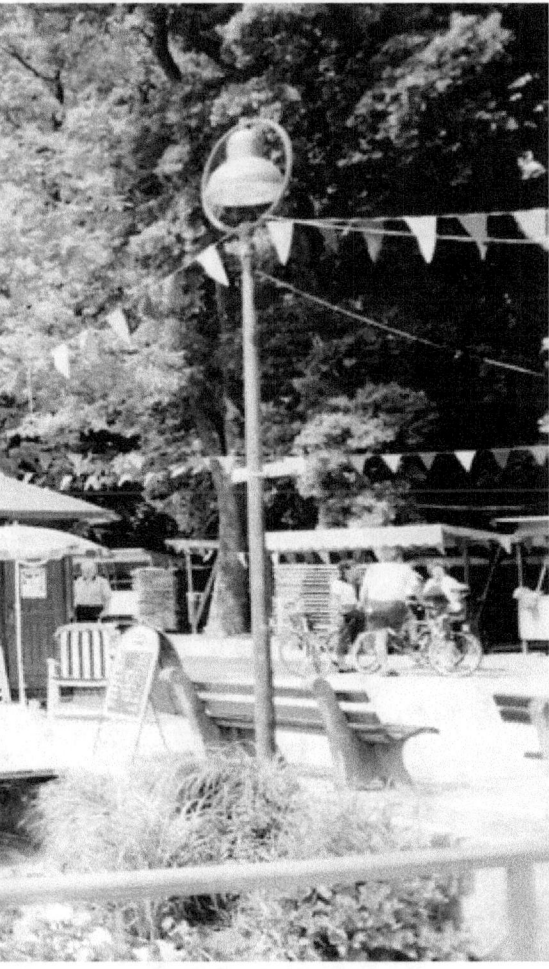

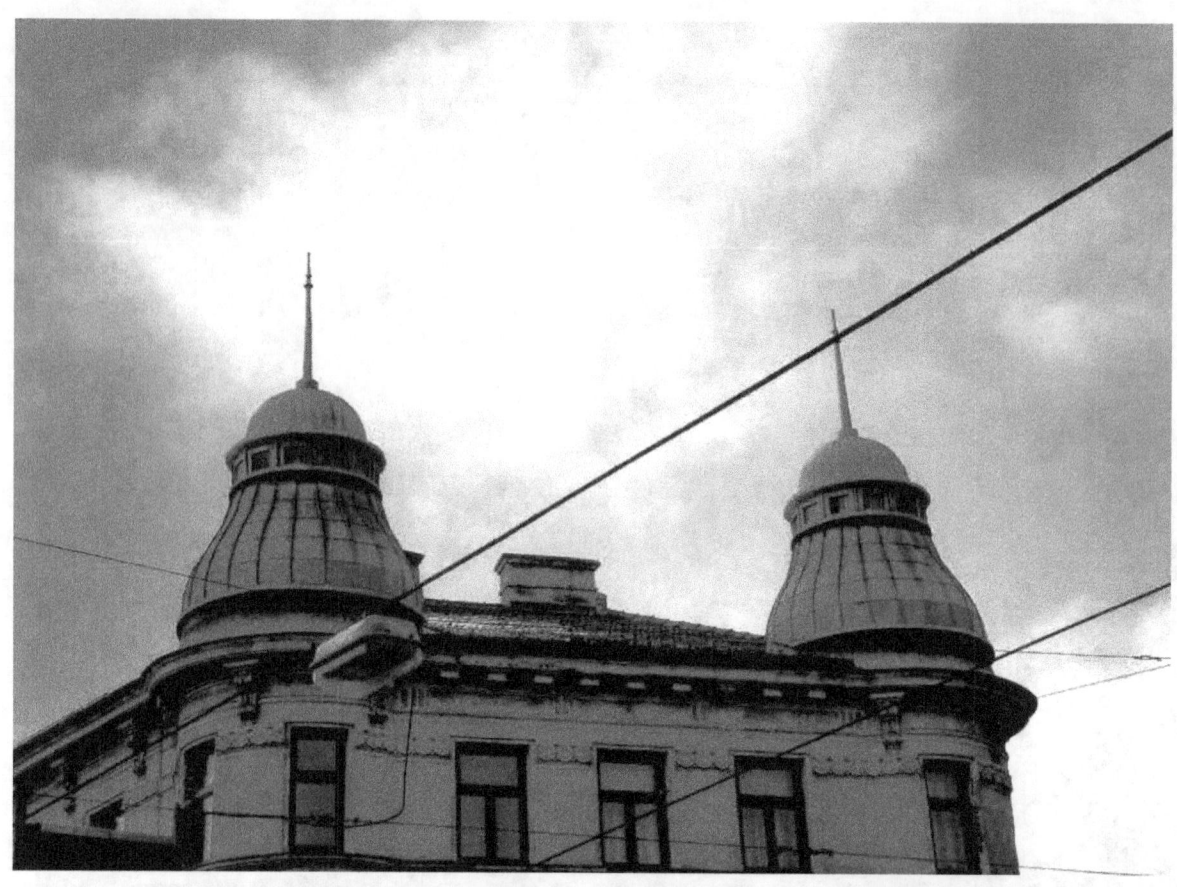

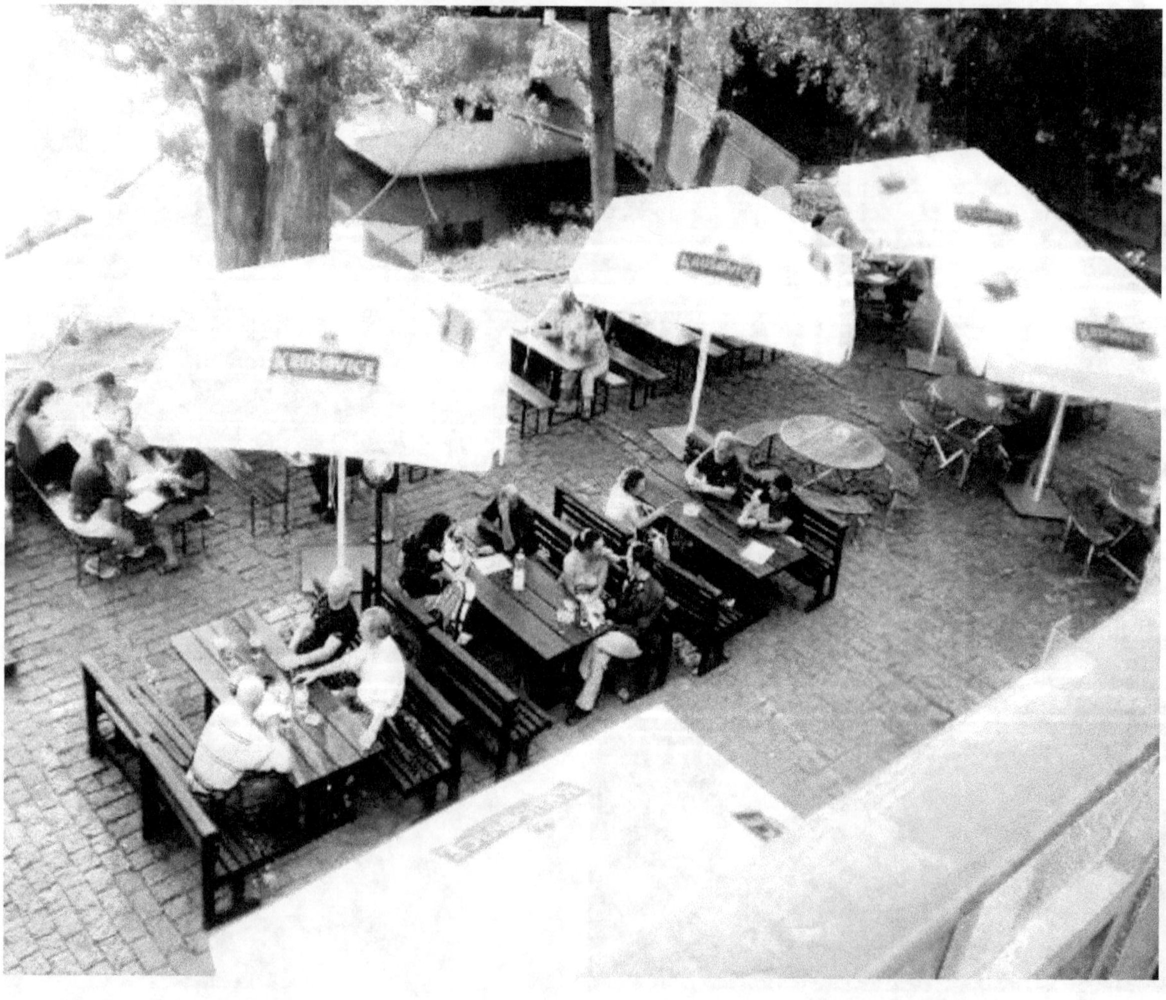

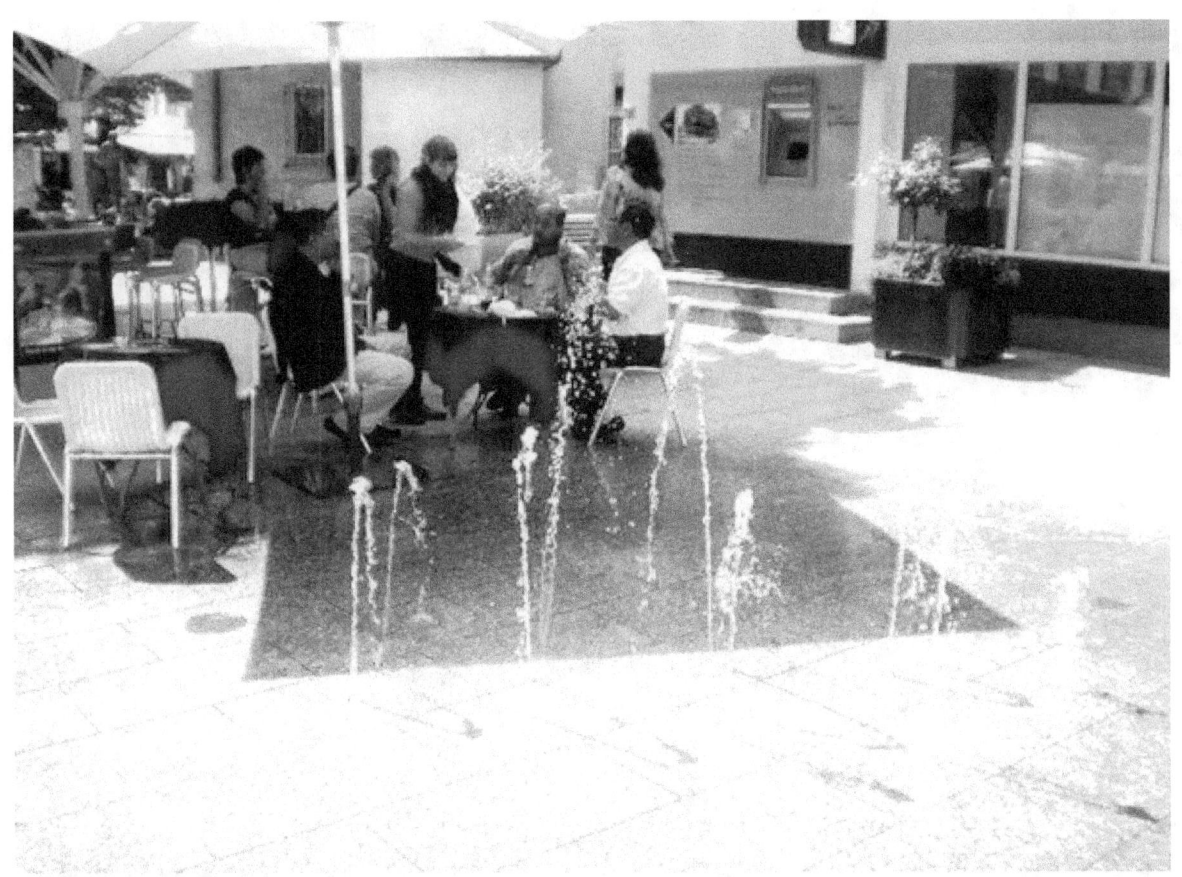

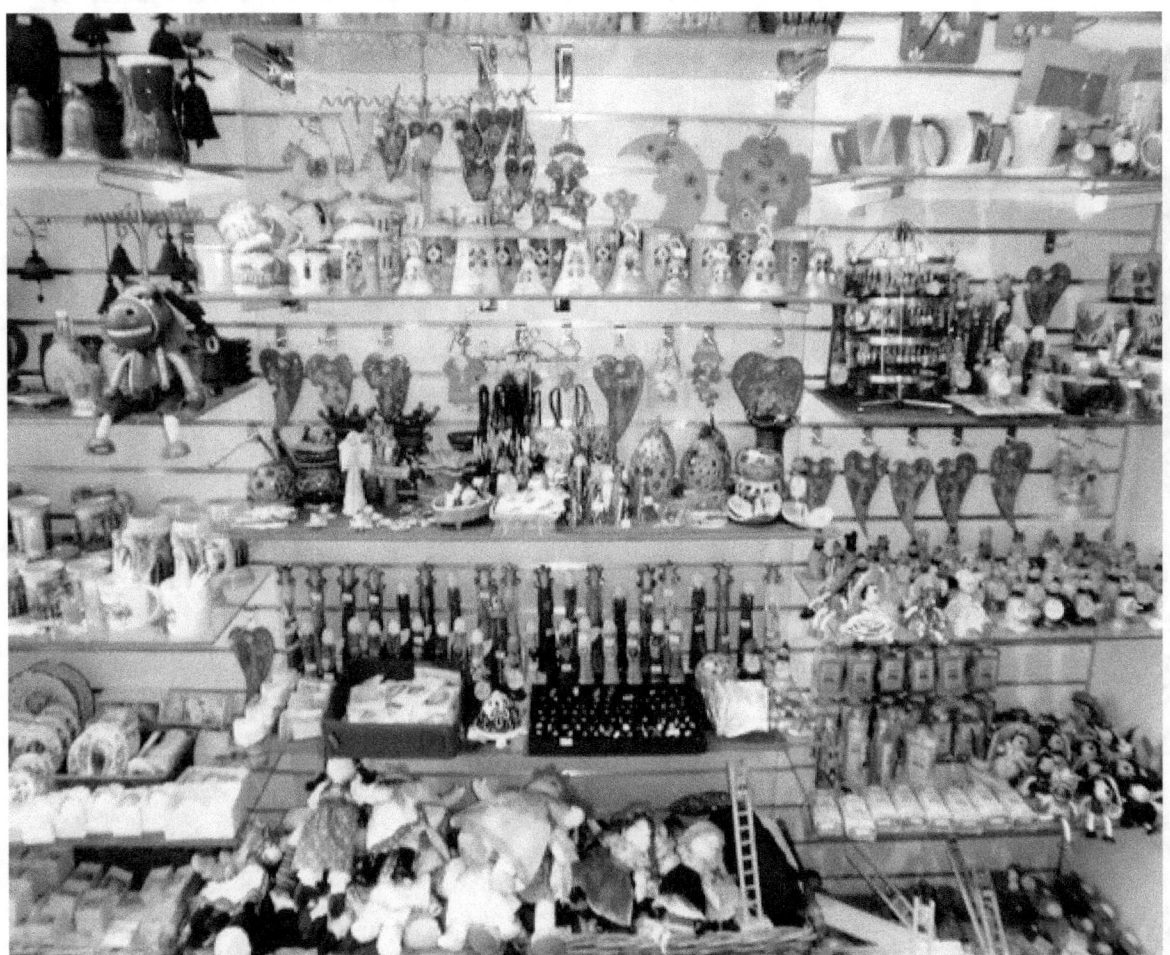

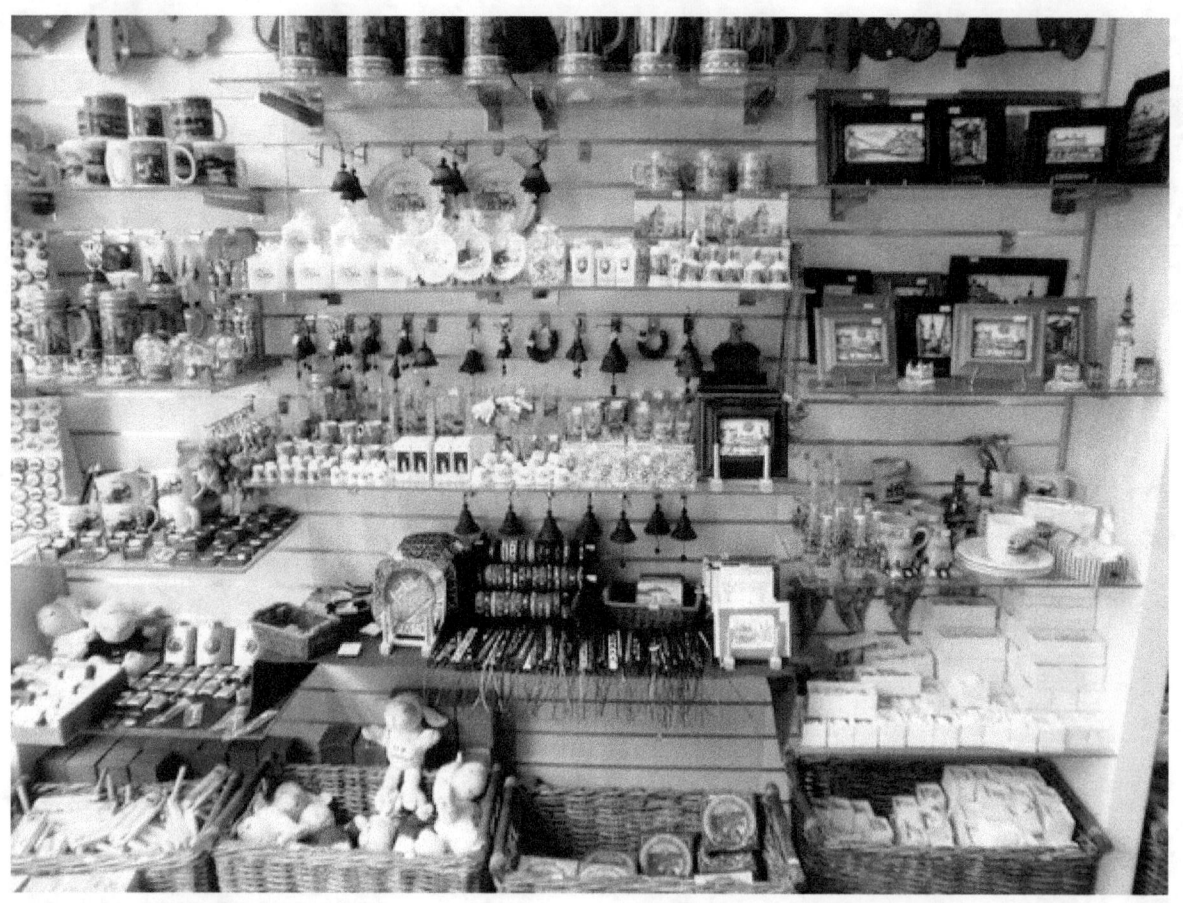

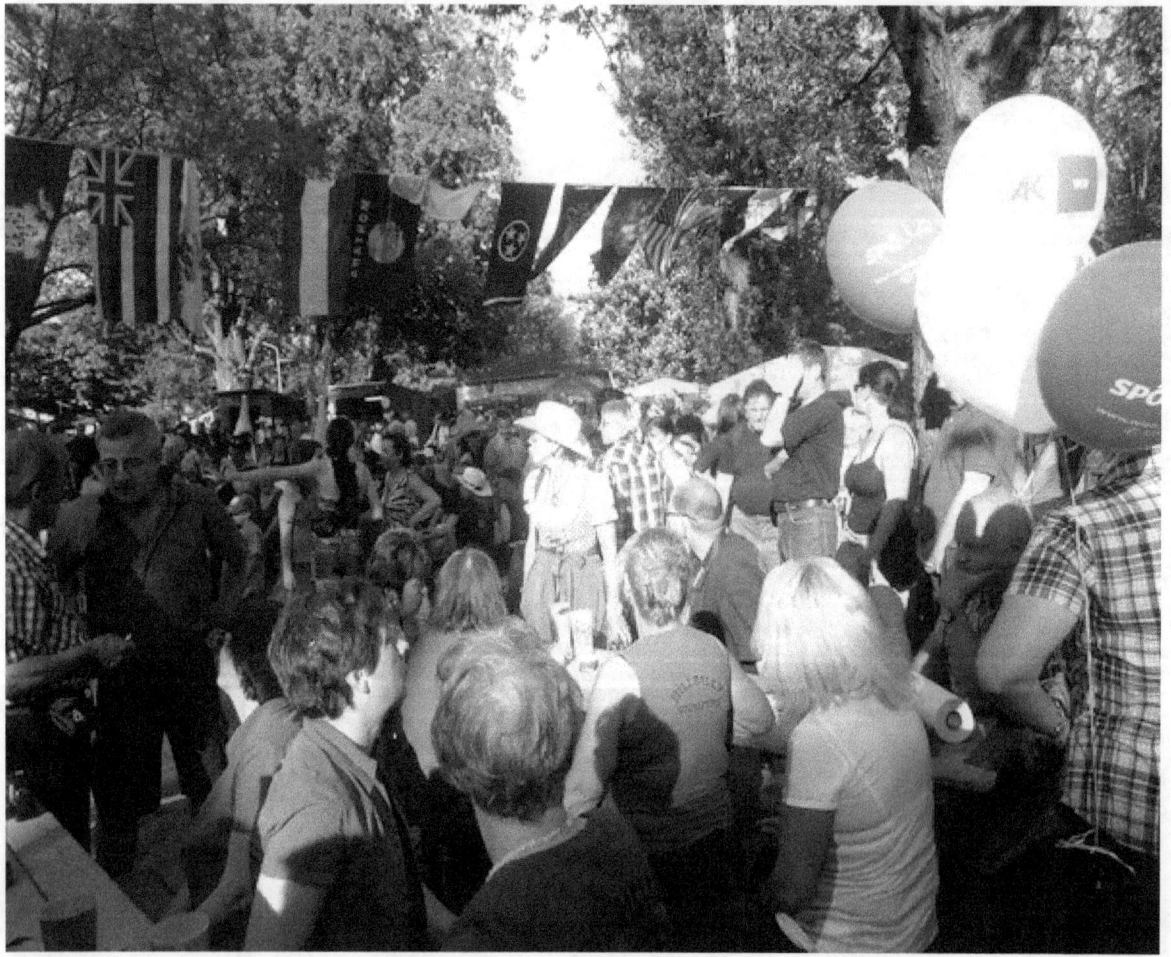

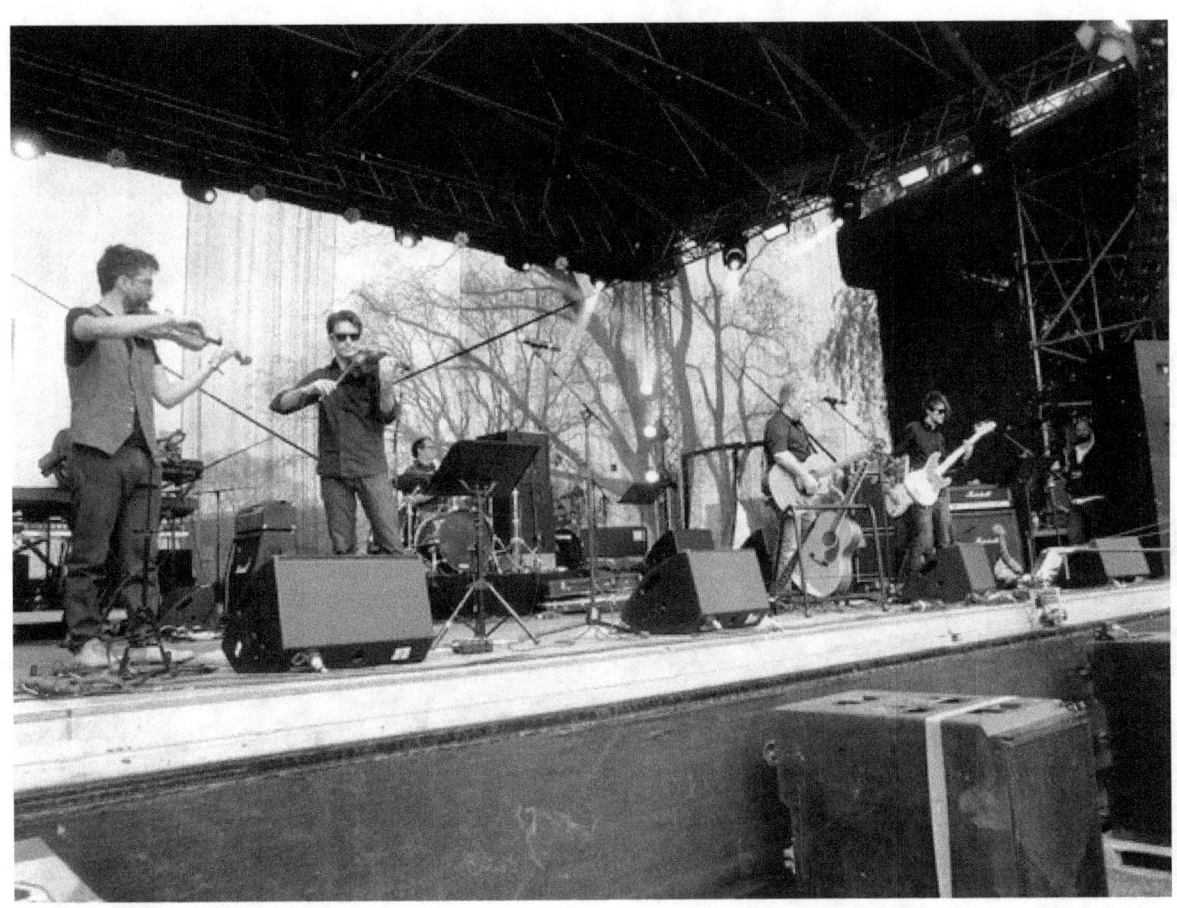

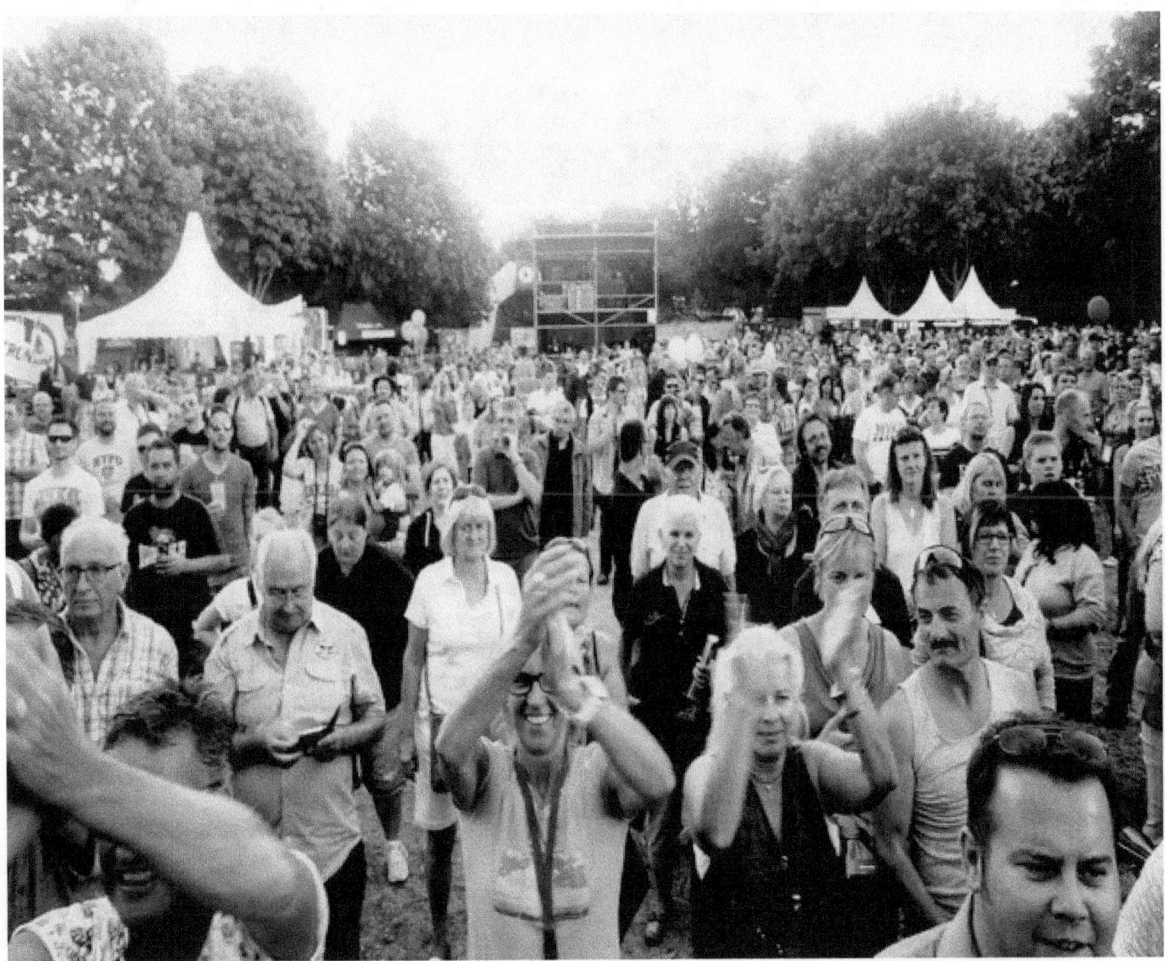

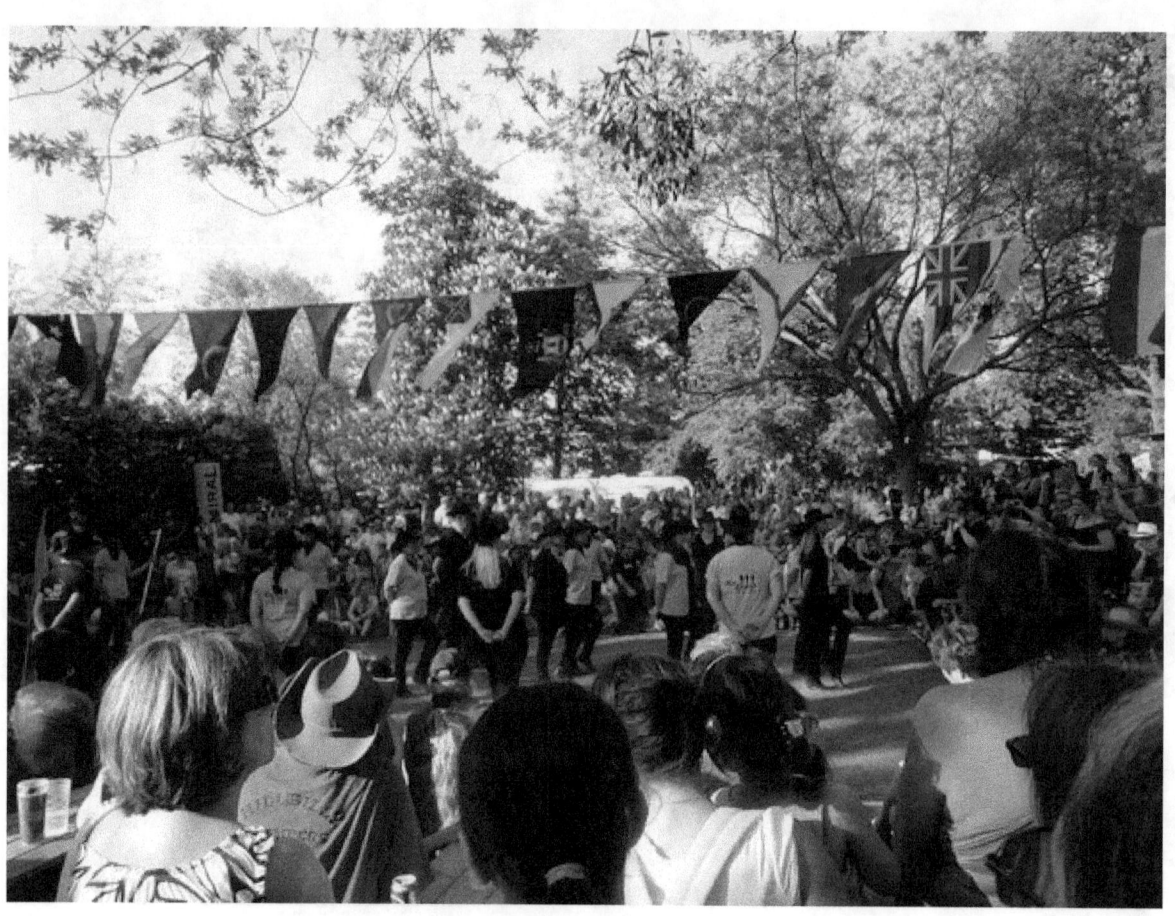

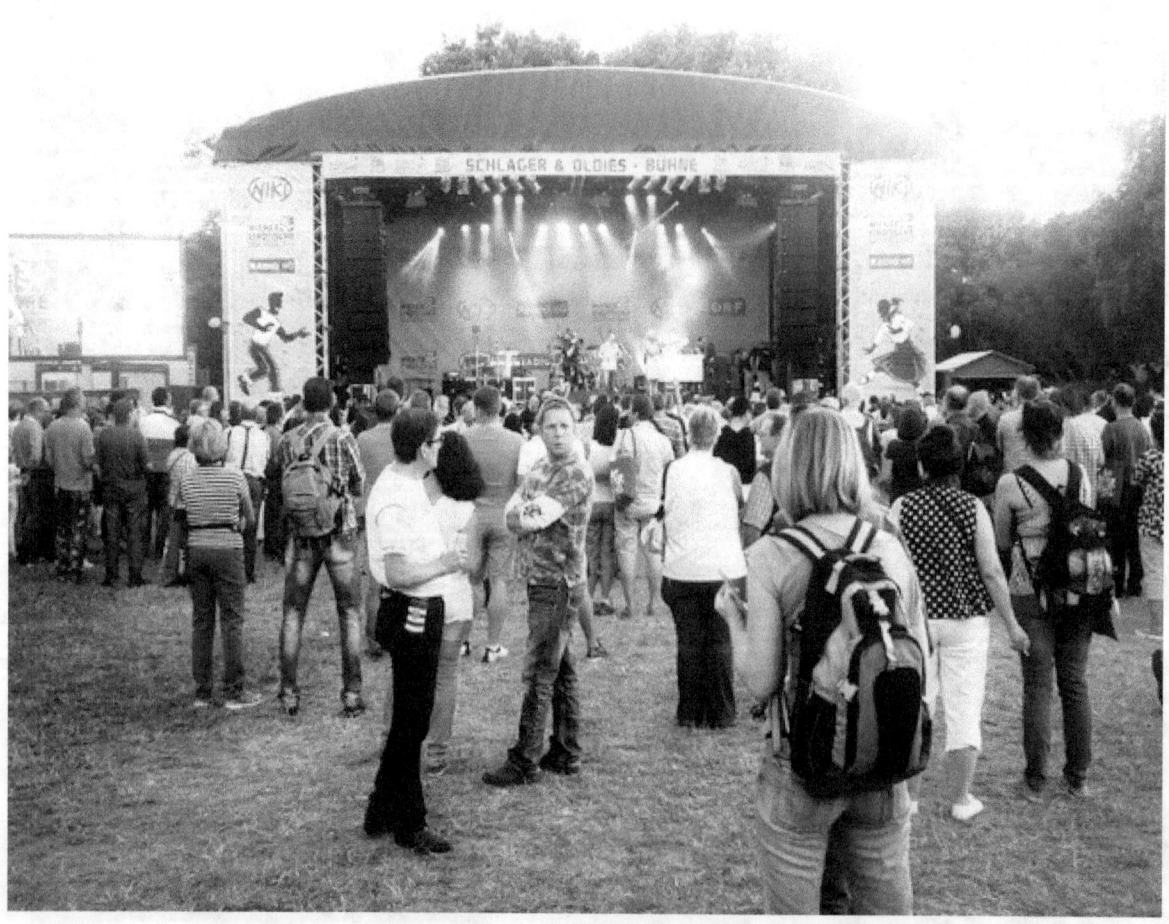

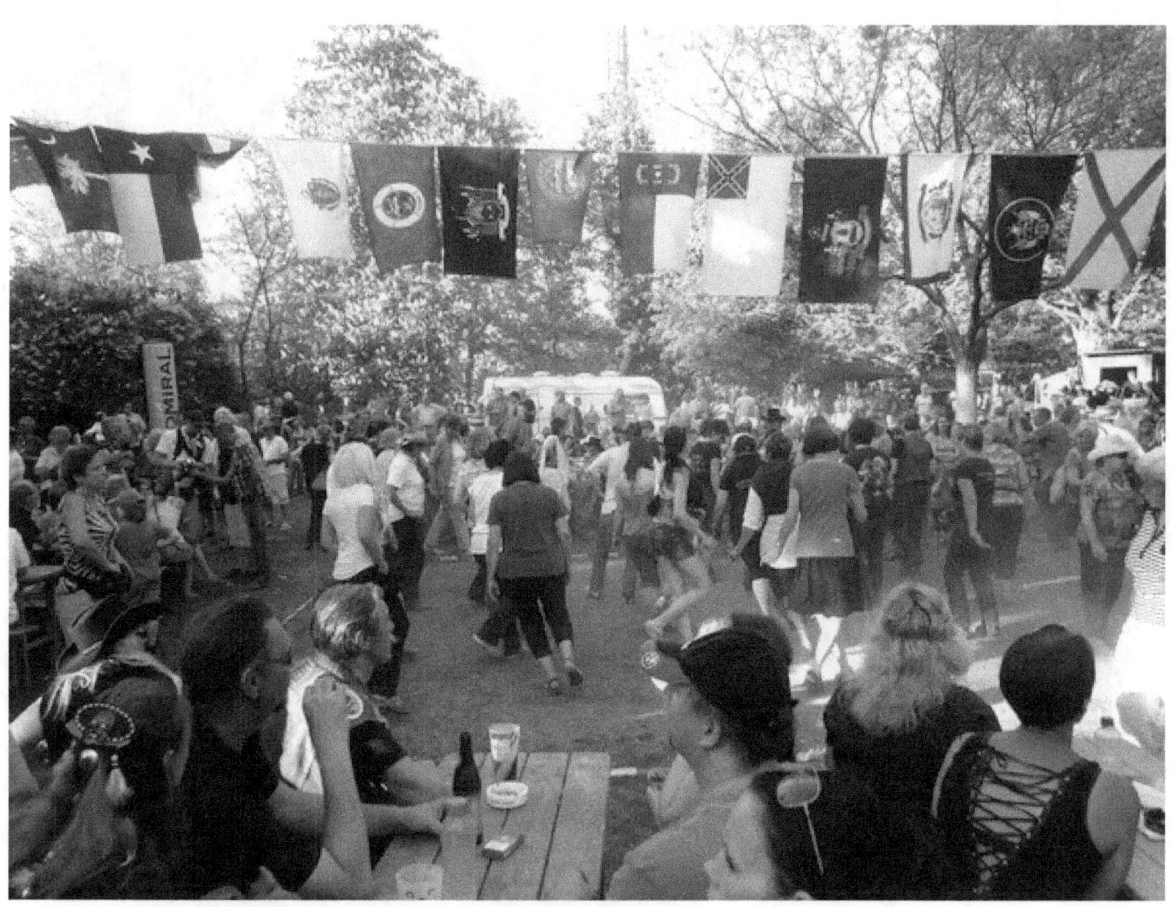

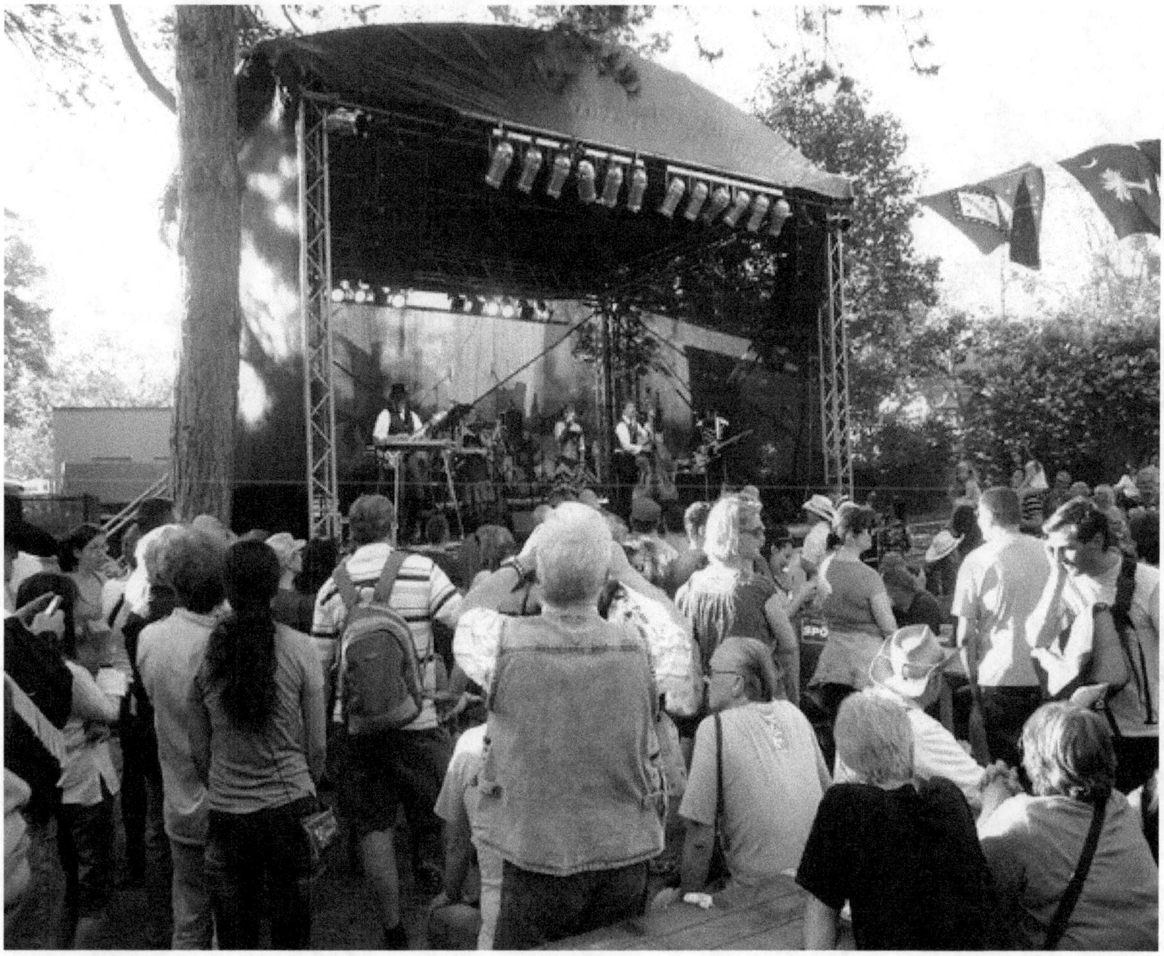

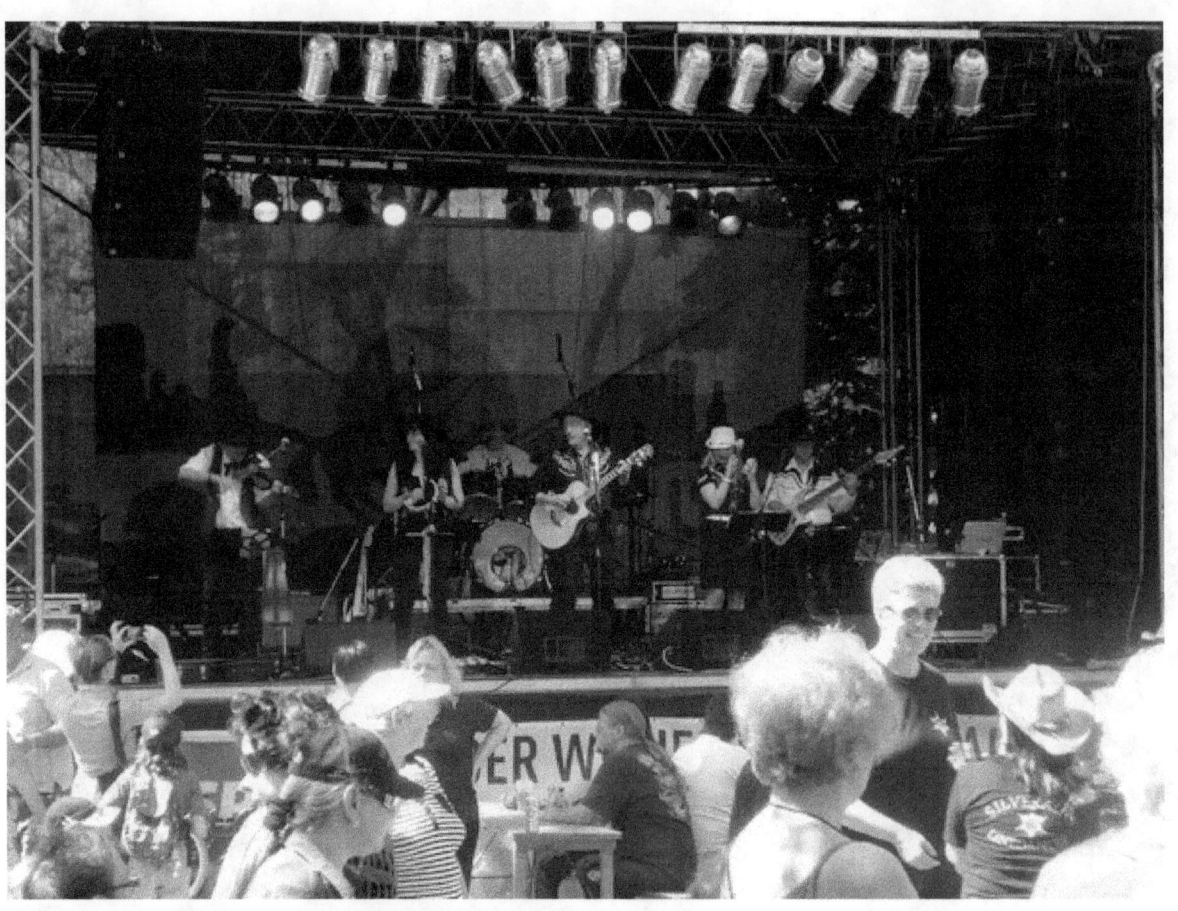

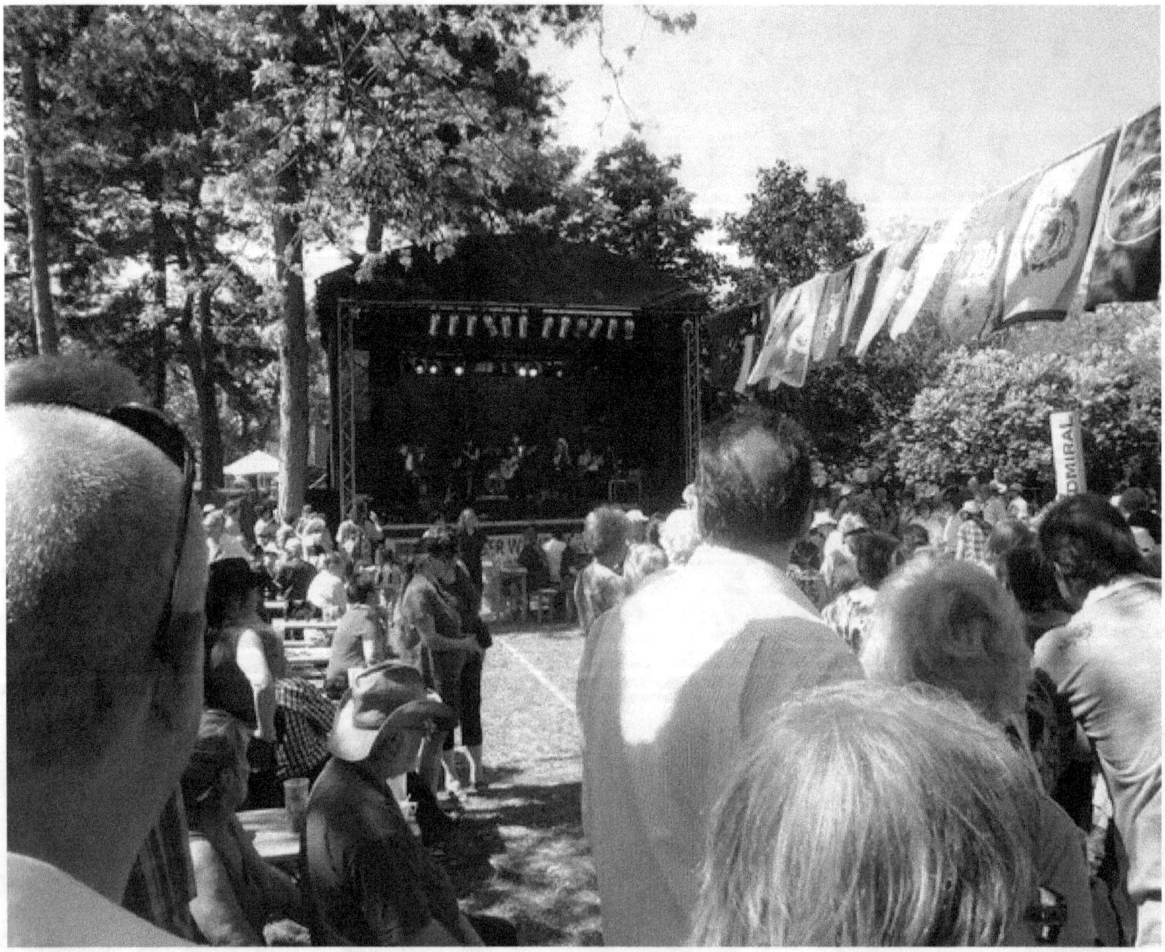

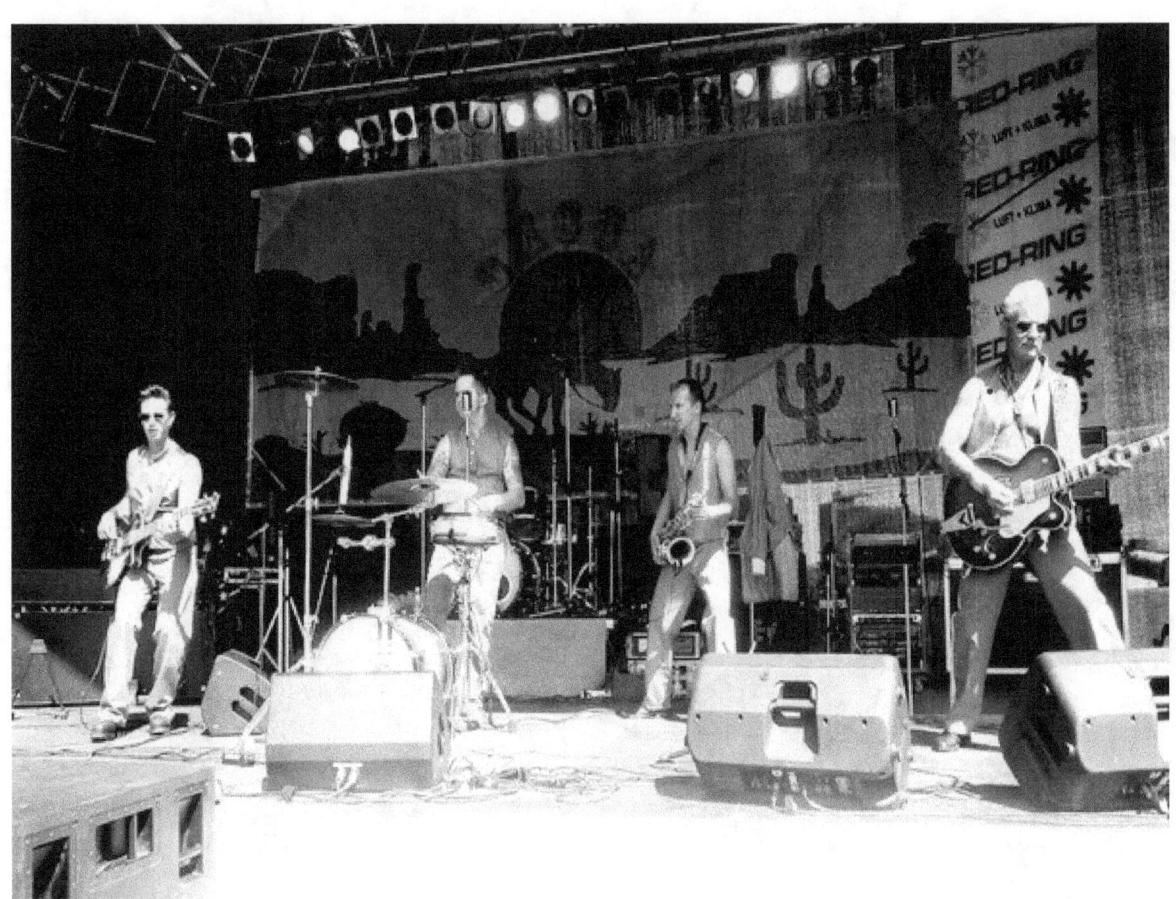

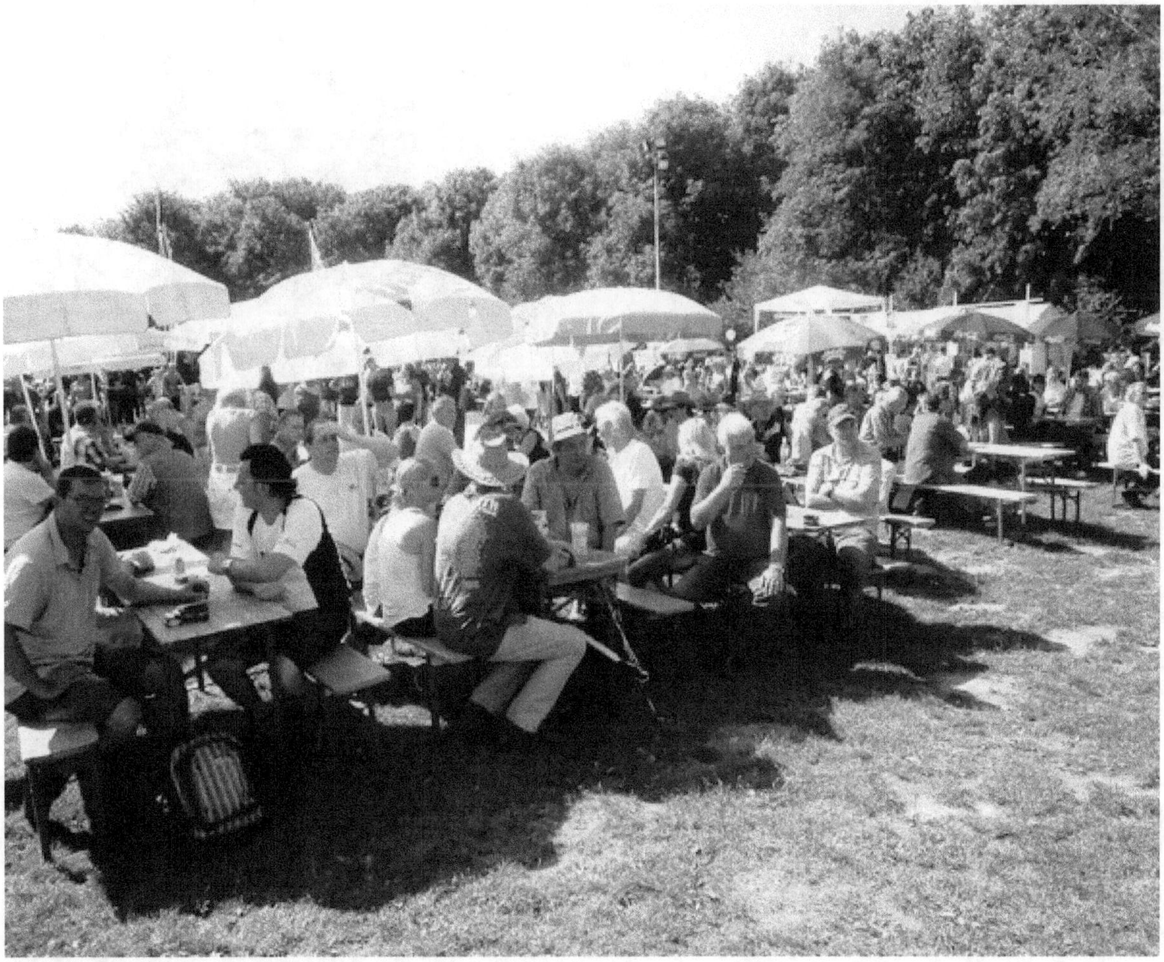

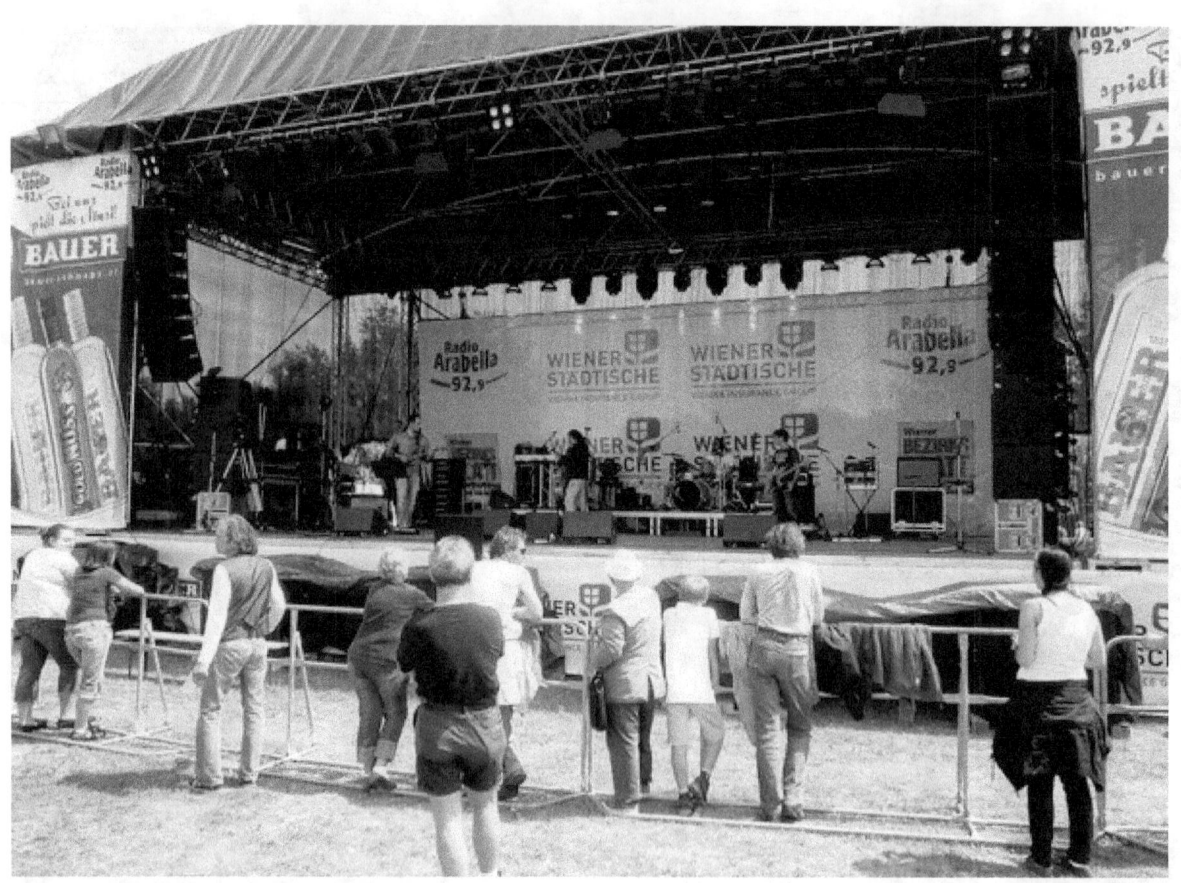

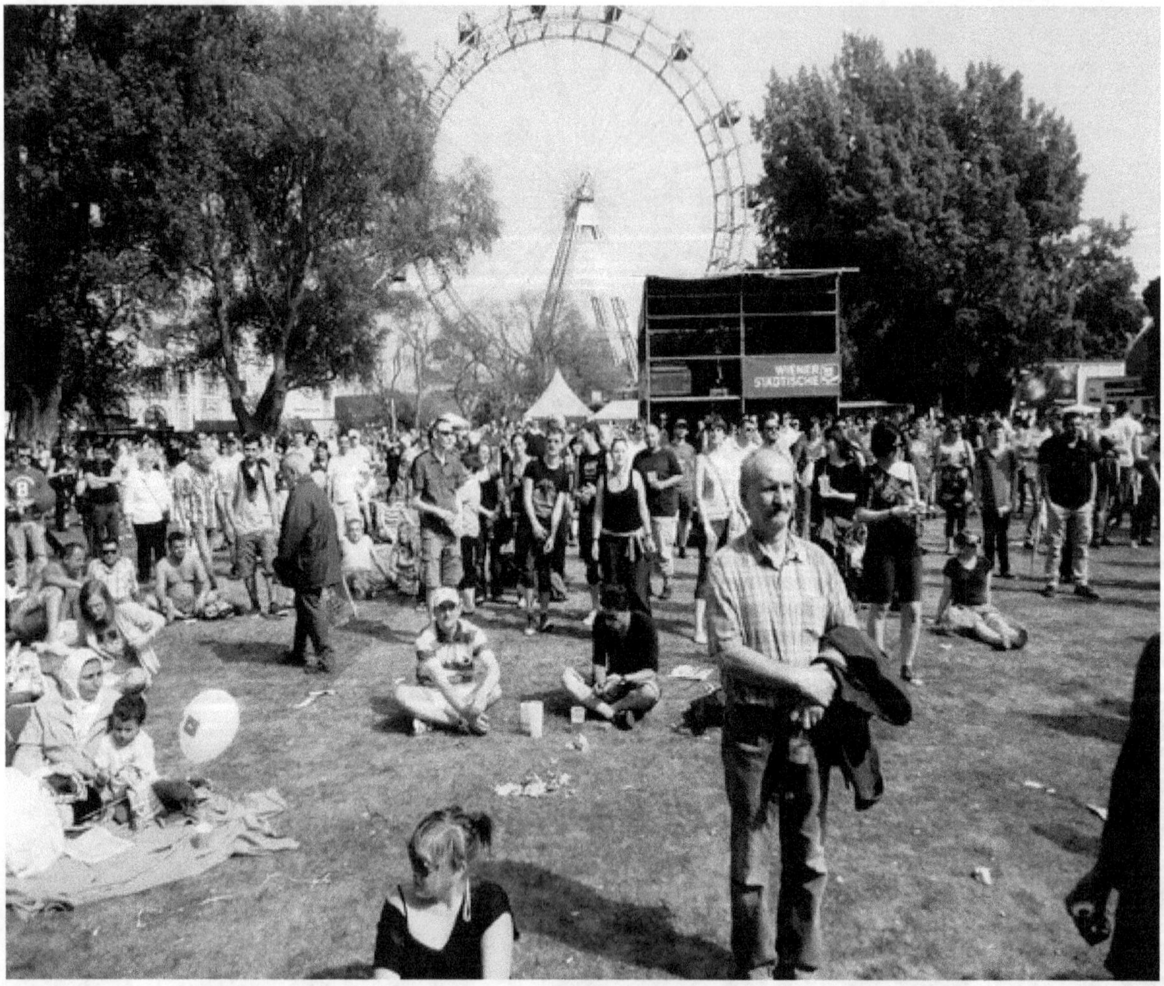

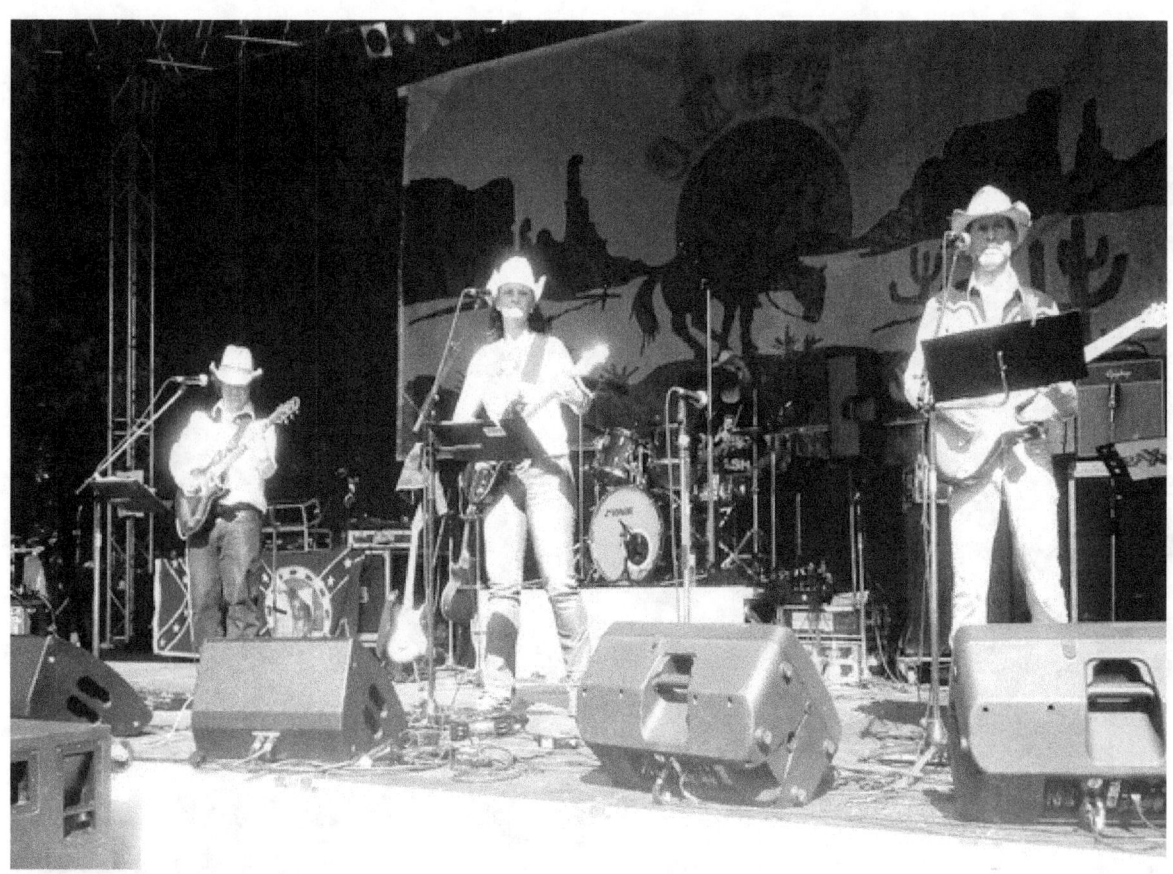

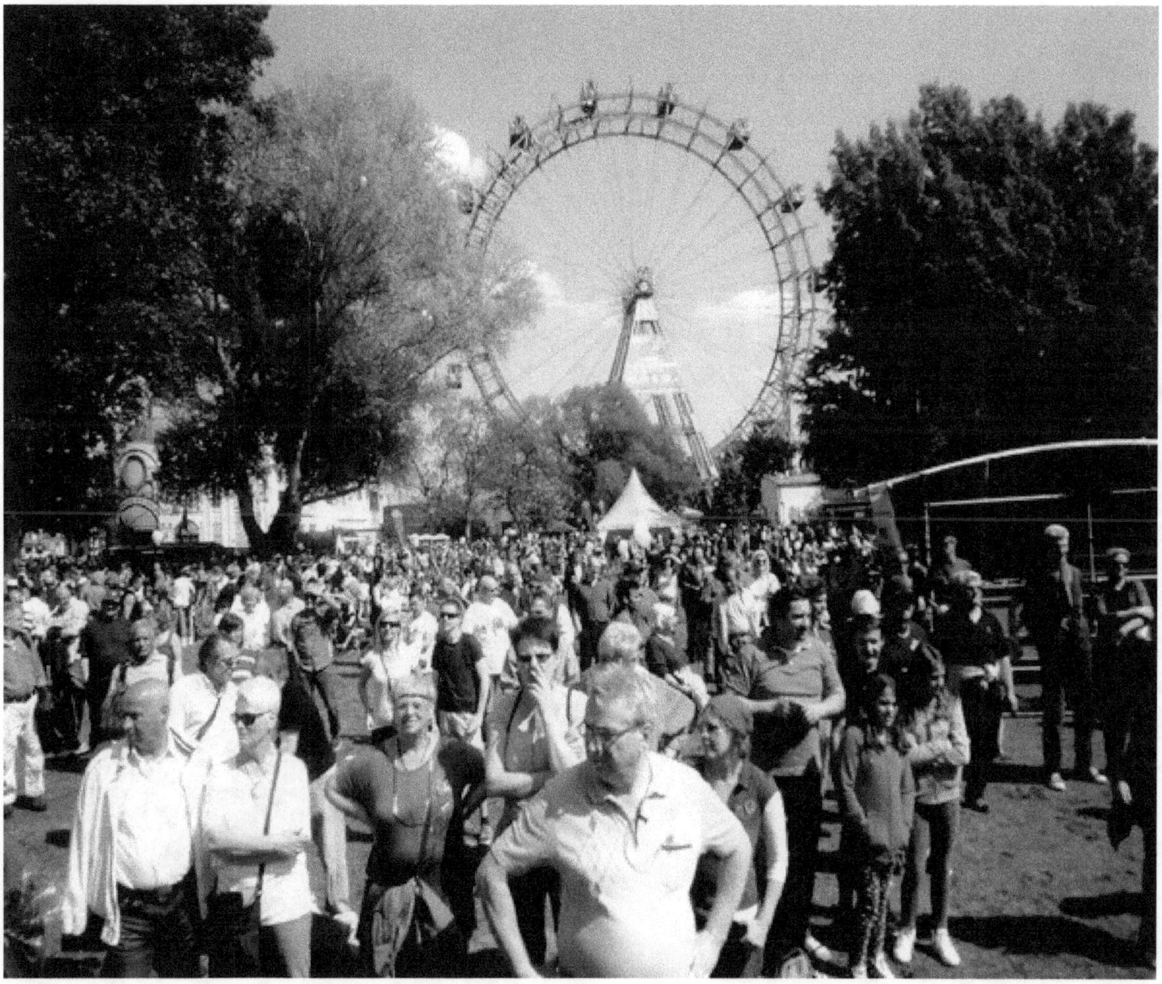

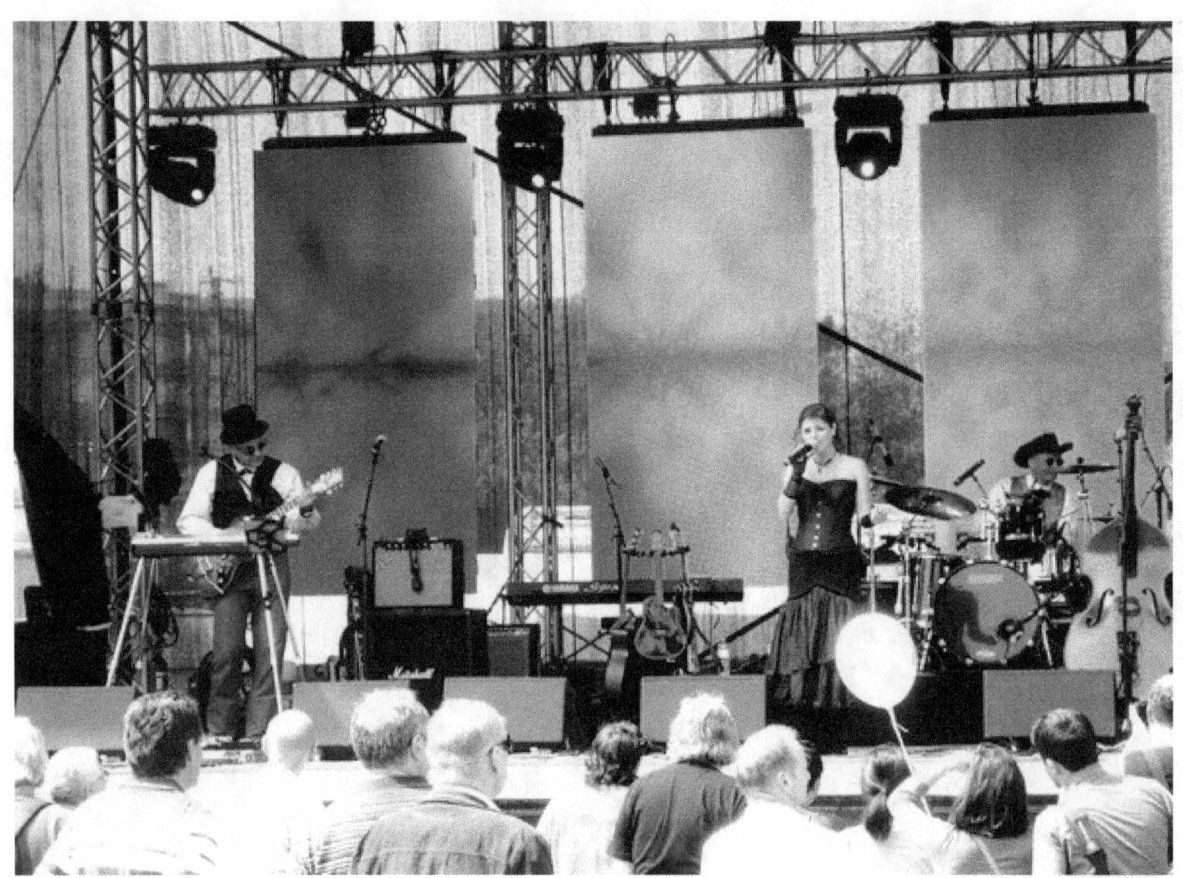

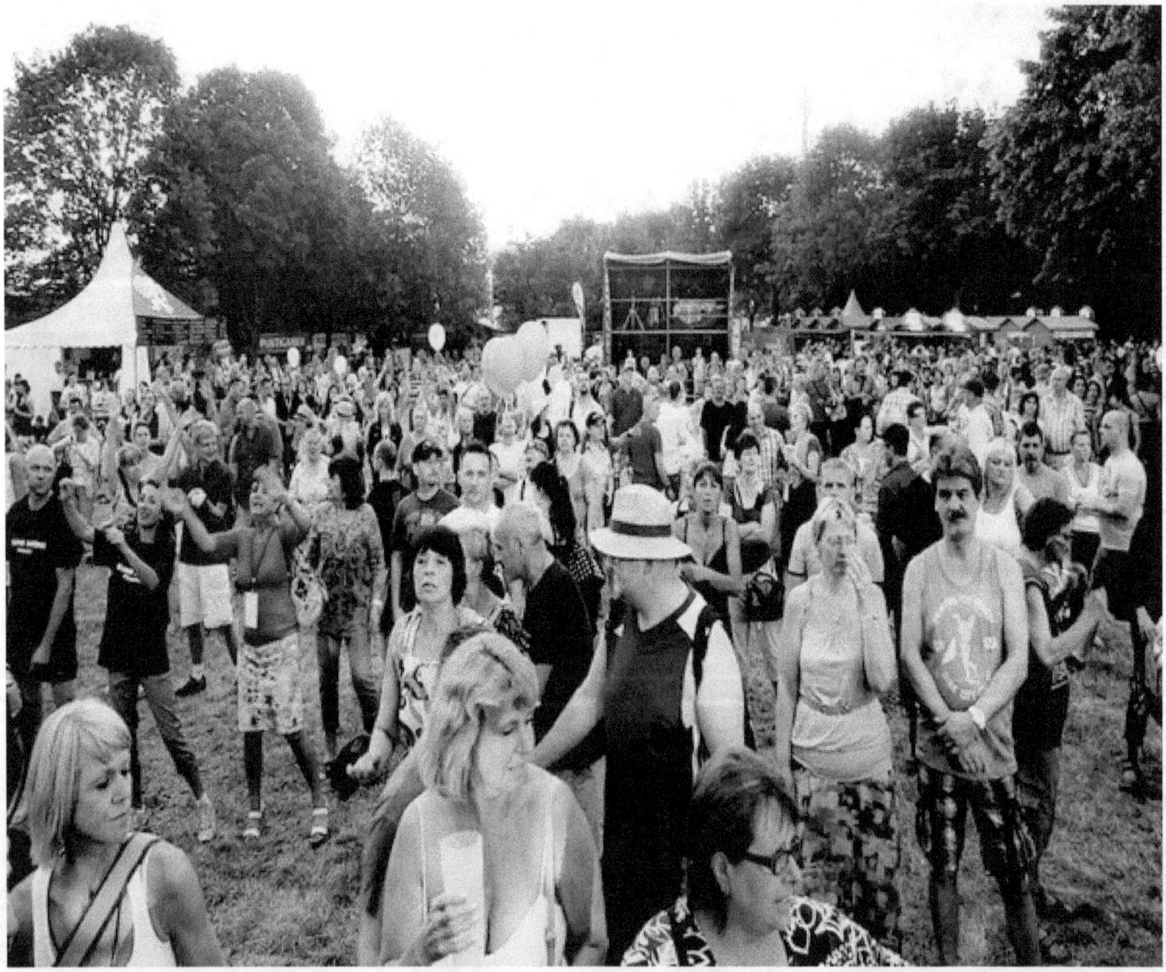

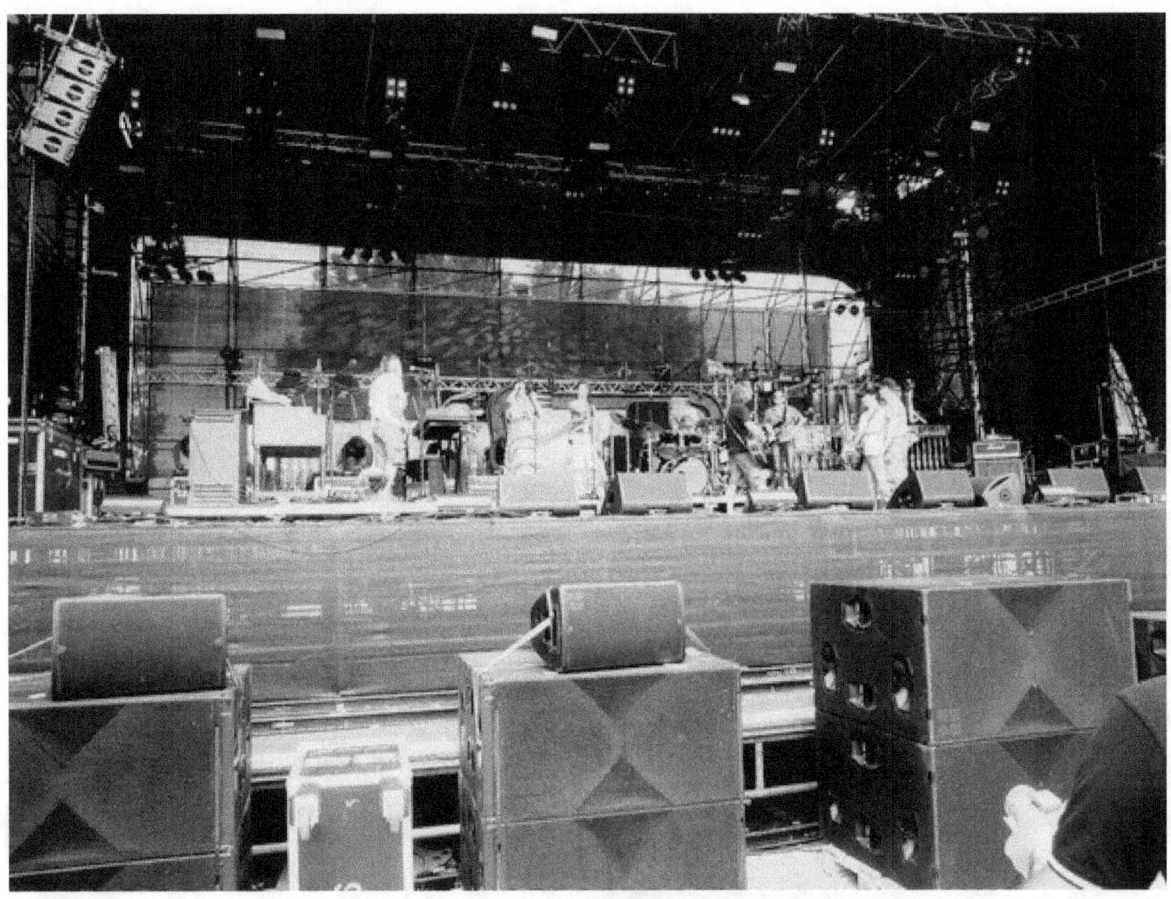

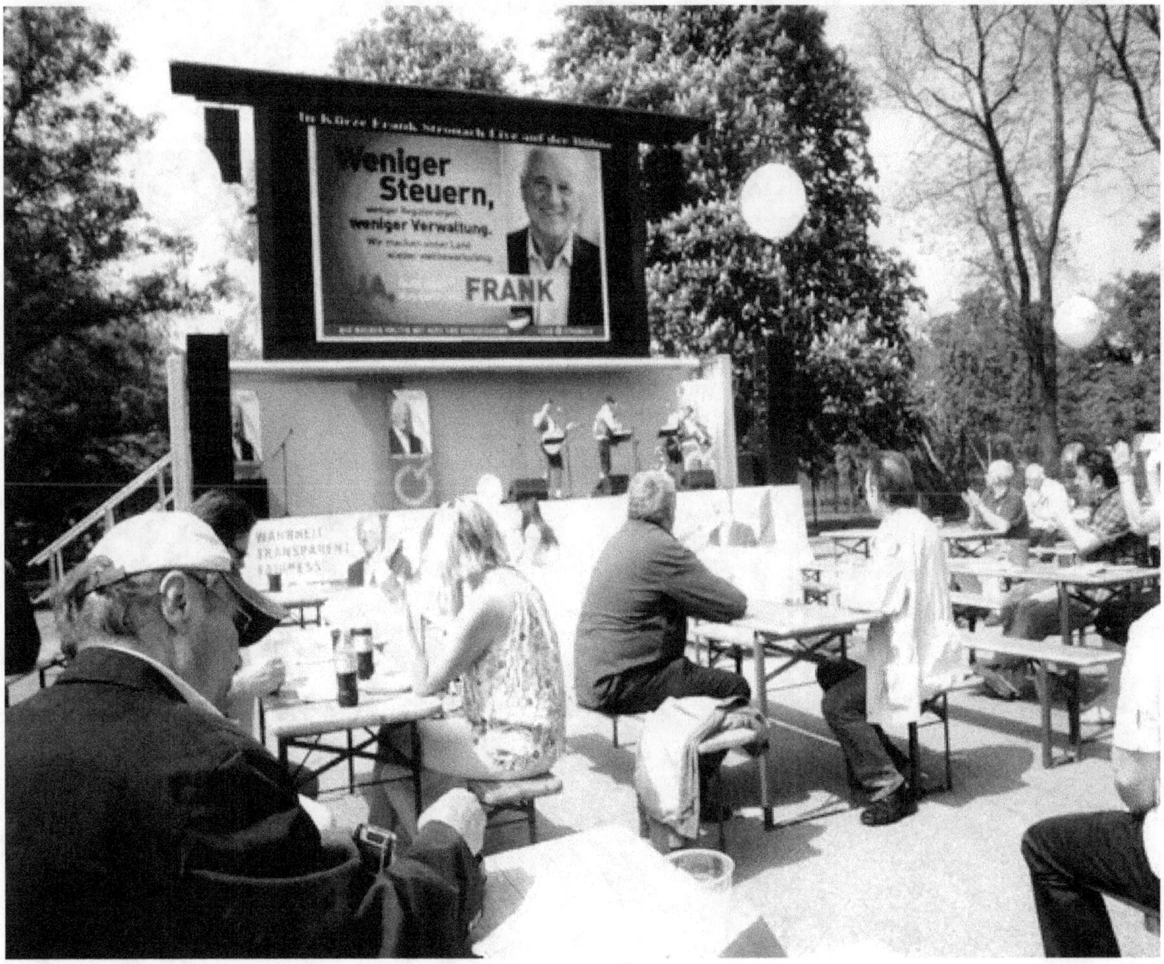

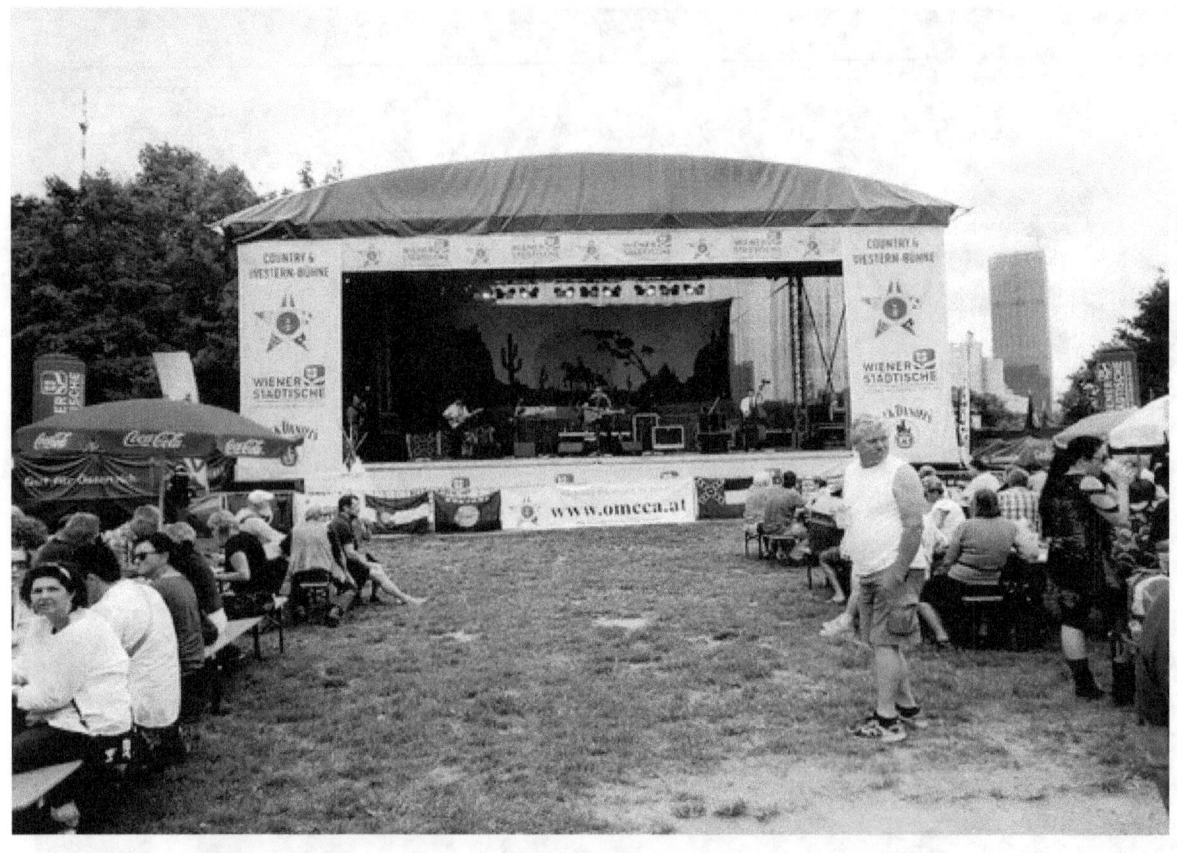

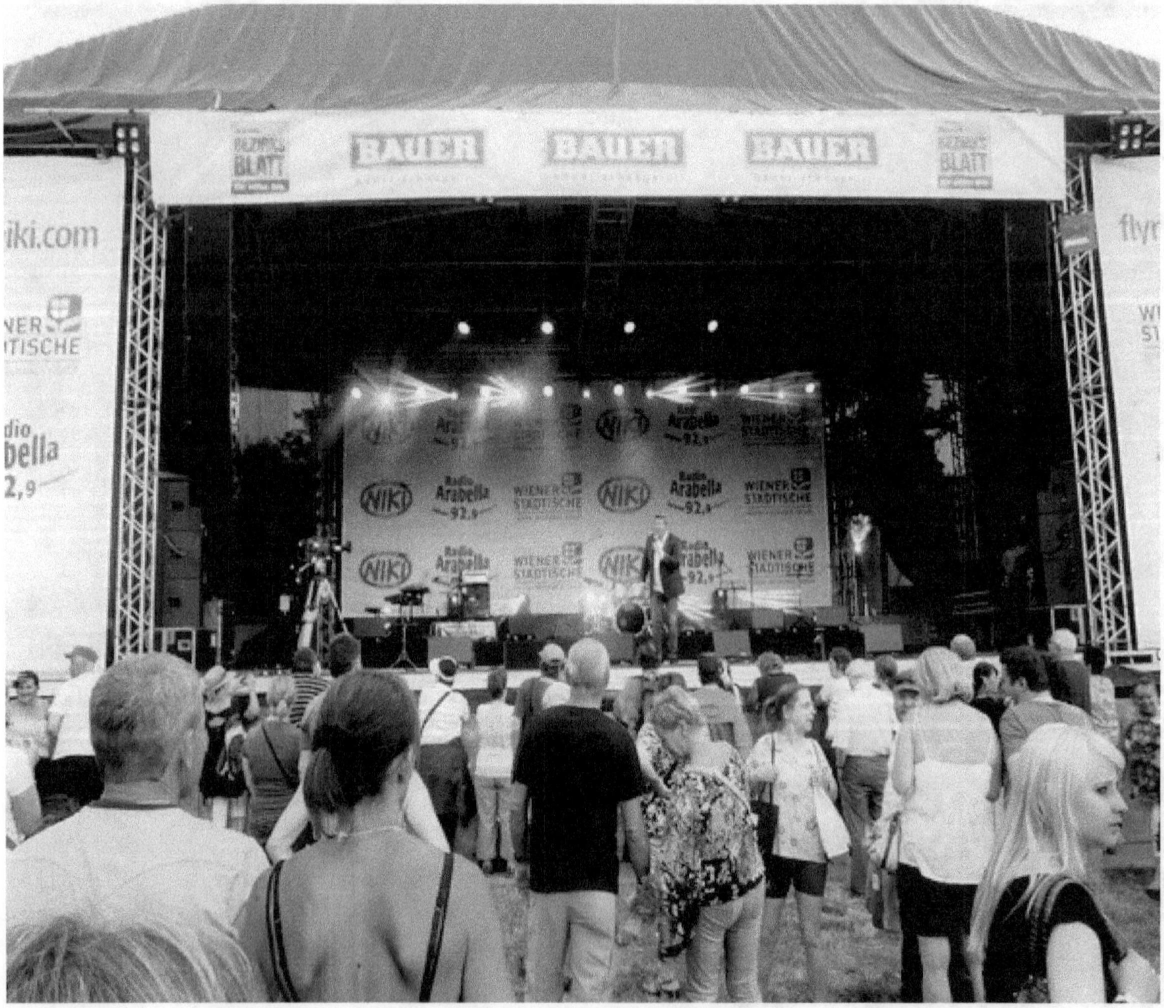

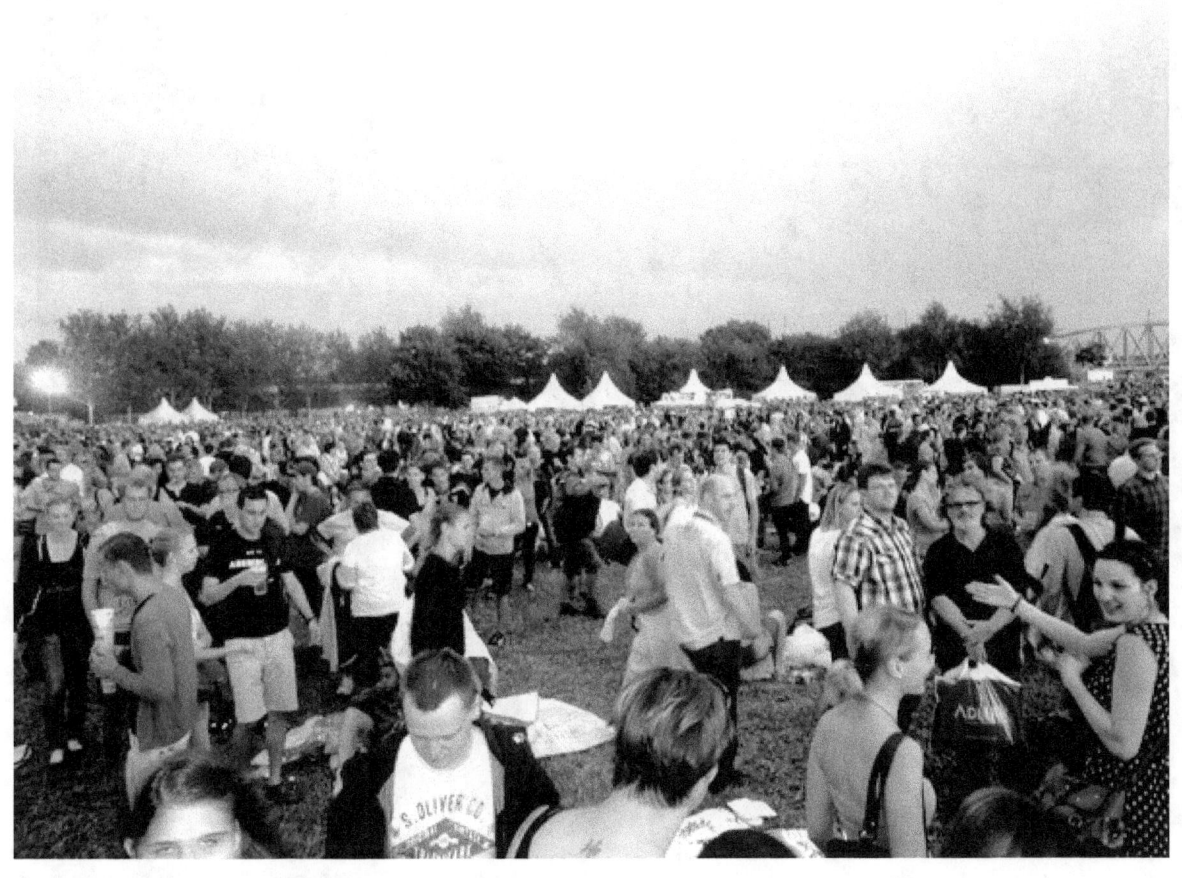

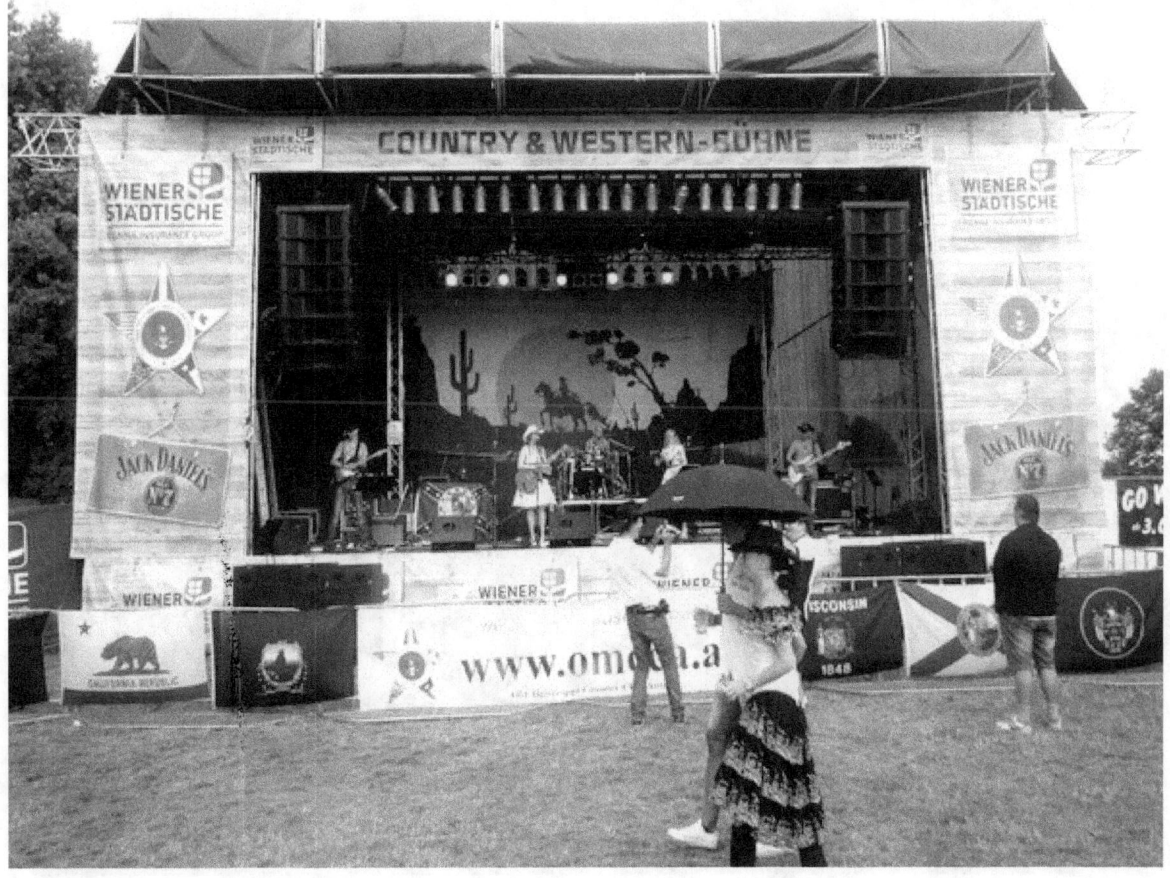

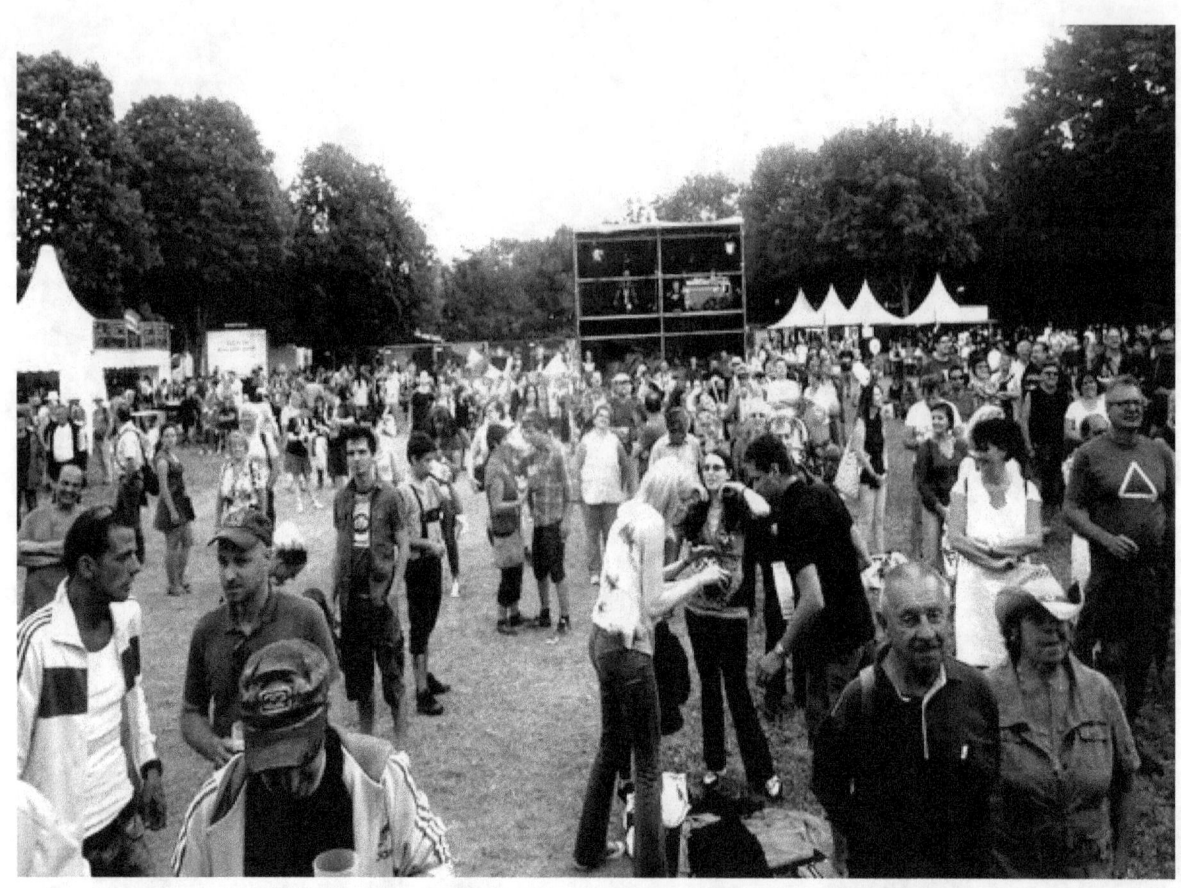

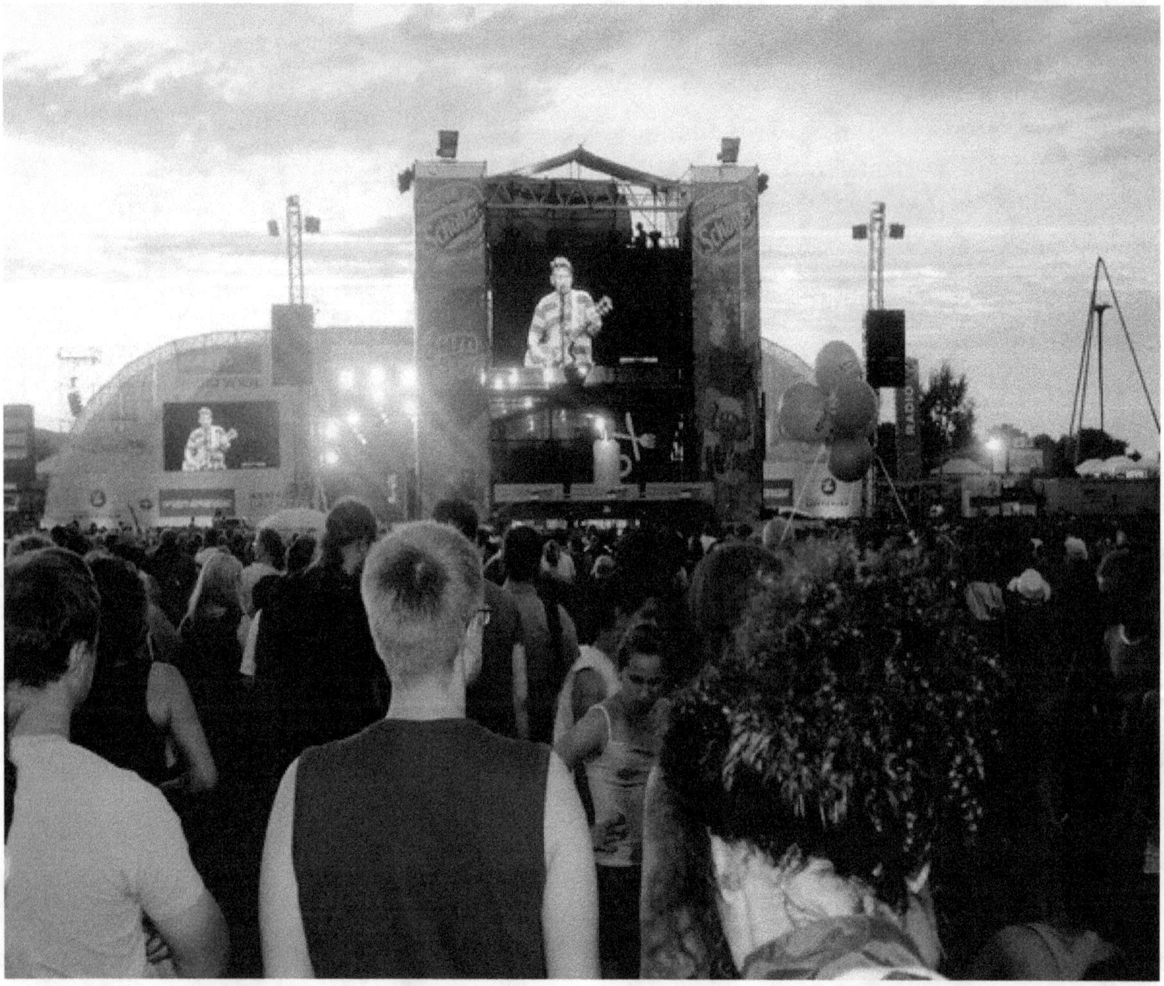

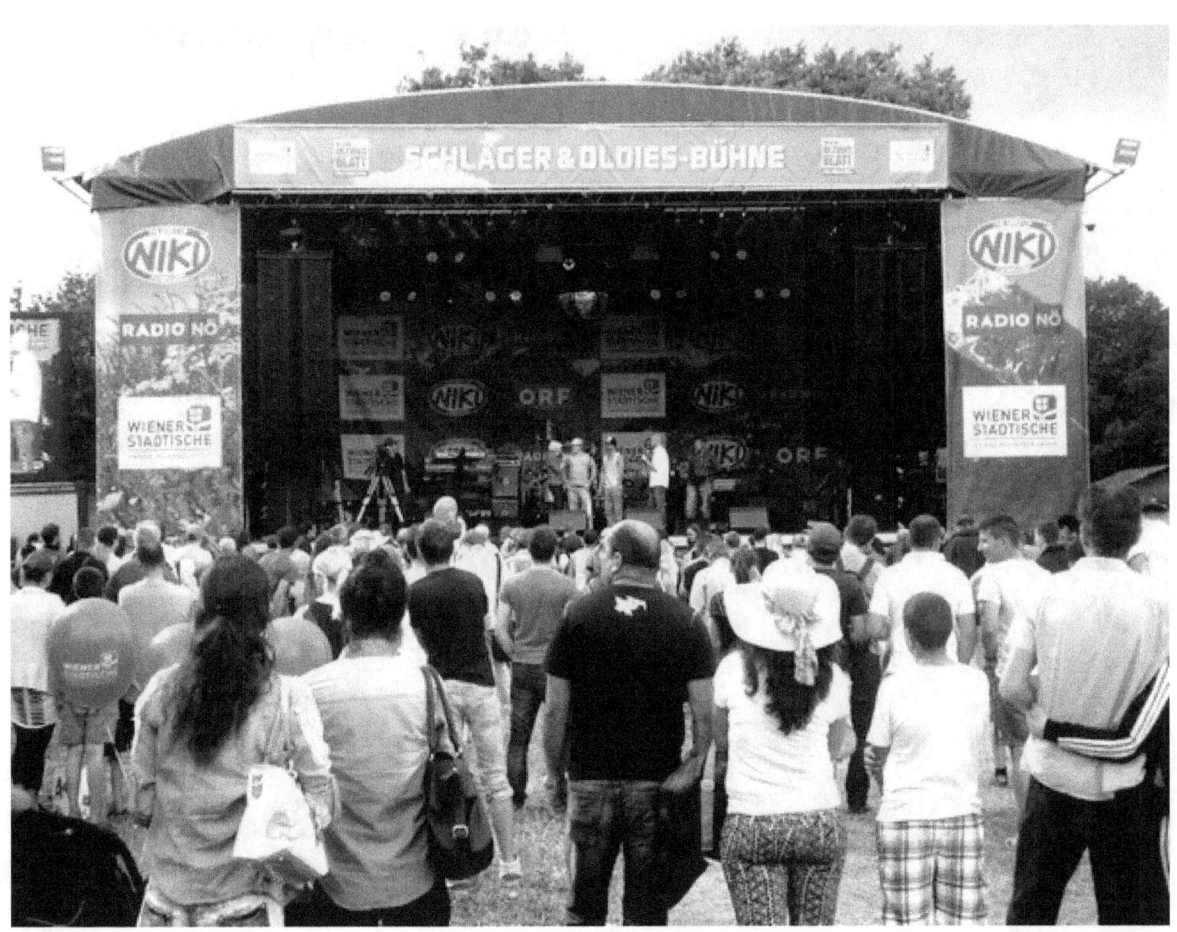

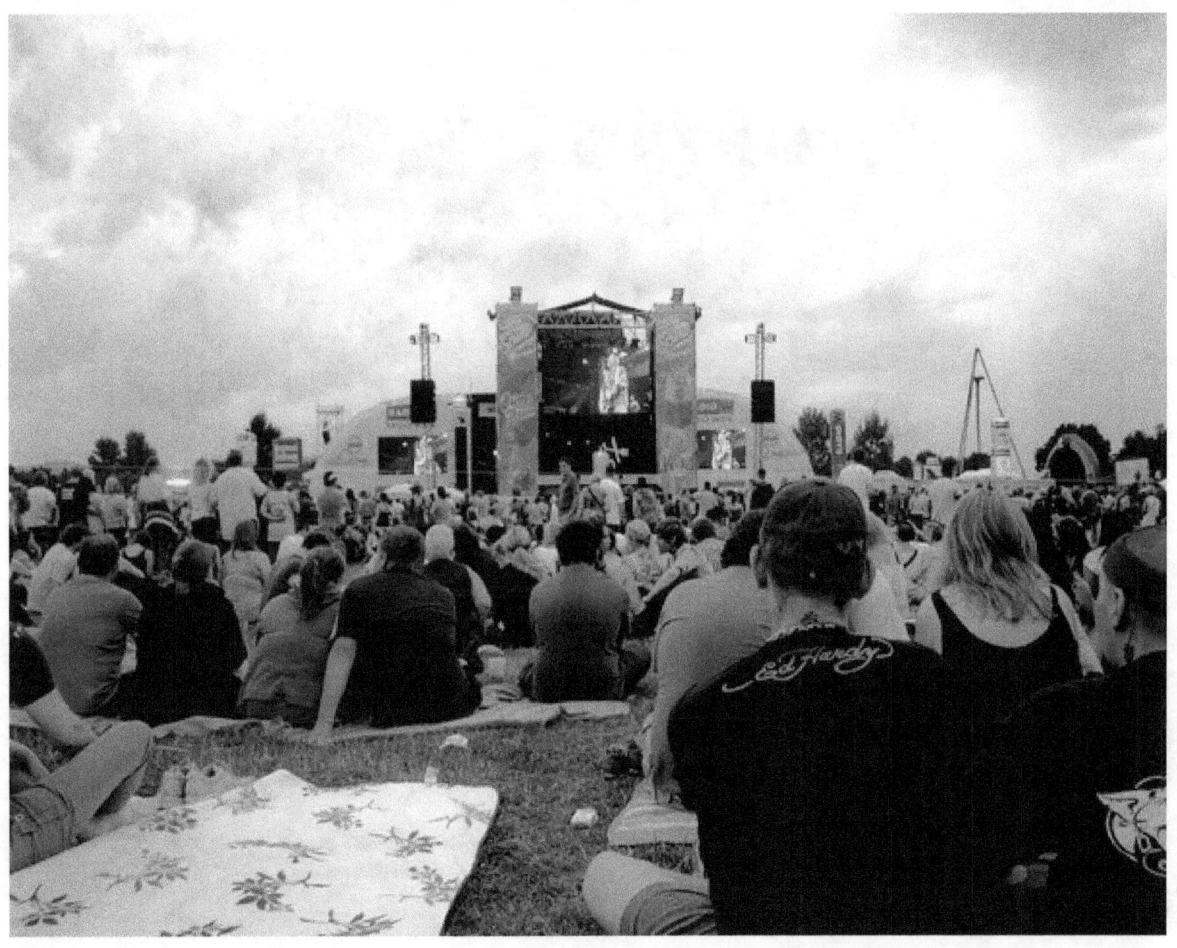

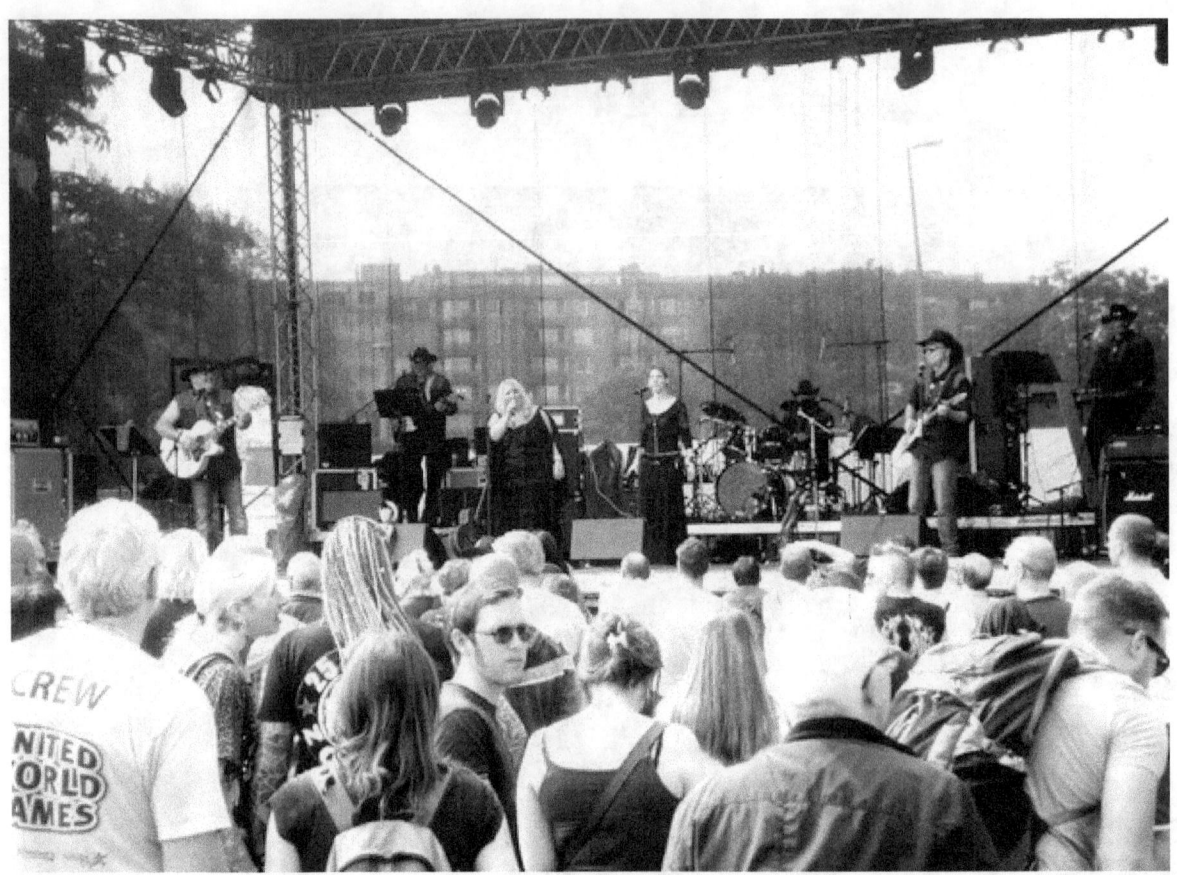

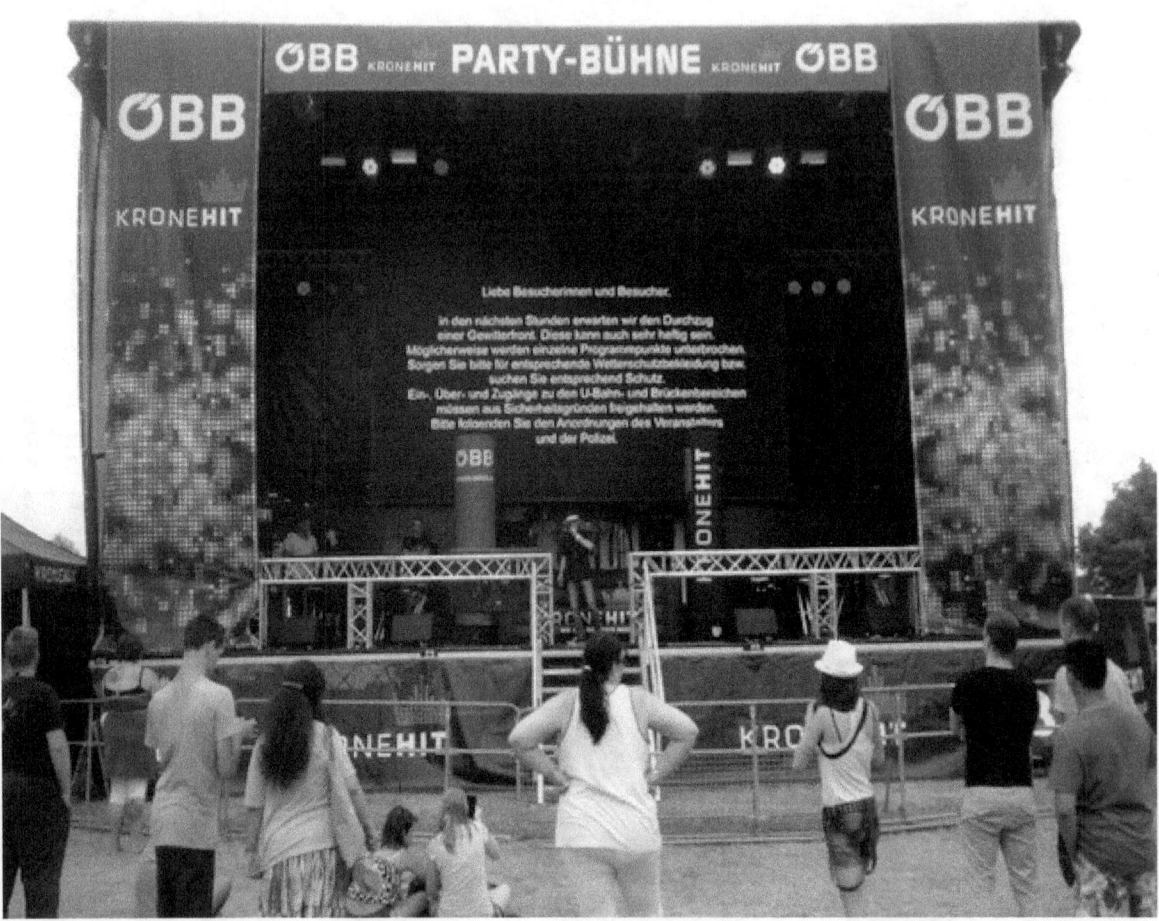

www.ingramcontent.com/pod-product-compliance
Lightning Source LLC
Chambersburg PA
CBHW080550190526

45169CB00007B/2712